Federal Reserve Bank of New York Staff Reports

Understanding the Securitization of Subprime Mortgage Credit

Adam B. Ashcraft
Til Schuermann

Staff Report no. 318
March 2008

This paper presents preliminary findings and is being distributed to economists and other interested readers solely to stimulate discussion and elicit comments. The views expressed in the paper are those of the authors and are not necessarily reflective of views at the Federal Reserve Bank of New York or the Federal Reserve System. Any errors or omissions are the responsibility of the authors.

(c) 2012 Booklife (Art and promotional copy only)
ISBN 978-1-300-05152-7

Commercially reprinted in 2012

This publication is subject to Title 17, United States Code, Sections 101 and 105. It is in the public domain and may not be

Understanding the Securitization of Subprime Mortgage Credit
Adam B. Ashcraft and Til Schuermann
Federal Reserve Bank of New York Staff Reports, no. 318
March 2008
JEL classification: G24, G28

Abstract

In this paper, we provide an overview of the subprime mortgage securitization process and the seven key informational frictions that arise. We discuss the ways that market participants work to minimize these frictions and speculate on how this process broke down. We continue with a complete picture of the subprime borrower and the subprime loan, discussing both predatory borrowing and predatory lending. We present the key structural features of a typical subprime securitization, document how rating agencies assign credit ratings to mortgage-backed securities, and outline how these agencies monitor the performance of mortgage pools over time. Throughout the paper, we draw upon the example of a mortgage pool securitized by New Century Financial during 2006.

Key words: subprime mortgage credit, securitization, rating agencies, principal agent, moral hazard

---

Ashcraft: Federal Reserve Bank of New York (e-mail: adam.ashcraft@ny.frb.org). Schuermann: Federal Reserve Bank of New York (e-mail: til.schuermann@ny.frb.org). The authors would like to thank Mike Holscher, Josh Frost, Alex LaTorre, Kevin Stiroh, and especially Beverly Hirtle for their valuable comments and contributions. The views expressed in this paper are those of the authors and do not necessarily reflect the position of the Federal Reserve Bank of New York or the Federal Reserve System.

Executive Summary

Section numbers containing more detail are provided in [square] brackets.

- Until very recently, the origination of mortgages and issuance of mortgage-backed securities (MBS) was dominated by loans to prime borrowers conforming to underwriting standards set by the Government Sponsored Agencies (GSEs) [2]
  - By 2006, non-agency origination of $1.480 trillion was more than 45% larger than agency origination, and non-agency issuance of $1.033 trillion was 14% larger than agency issuance of $905 billion.

- The securitization process is subject to seven key frictions.
  1) Fictions between the mortgagor and the originator: predatory lending [2.1.1]
     - Subprime borrowers can be financially unsophisticated
     - Resolution: federal, state, and local laws prohibiting certain lending practices, as well as the recent regulatory guidance on subprime lending
  2) Frictions between the originator and the arranger: Predatory borrowing and lending [2.1.2]
     - The originator has an information advantage over the arranger with regard to the quality of the borrower.
     - Resolution: due diligence of the arranger. Also the originator typically makes a number of representations and warranties (R&W) about the borrower and the underwriting process. When these are violated, the originator generally must repurchase the problem loans.
  3) Frictions between the arranger and third-parties: Adverse selection [2.1.3]
     - The arranger has more information about the quality of the mortgage loans which creates an adverse selection problem: the arranger can securitize bad loans (the lemons) and keep the good ones. This third friction in the securitization of subprime loans affects the relationship that the arranger has with the warehouse lender, the credit rating agency (CRA), and the asset manager.
     - Resolution: haircuts on the collateral imposed by the warehouse lender. Due diligence conducted by the portfolio manager on the arranger and originator. CRAs have access to some private information; they have a franchise value to protect.
  4) Frictions between the servicer and the mortgagor: Moral hazard [2.1.4]
     - In order to maintain the value of the underlying asset (the house), the mortgagor (borrower) has to pay insurance and taxes on and generally maintain the property. In the approach to and during delinquency, the mortgagor has little incentive to do all that.
     - Resolution: Require the mortgagor to regularly escrow funds for both insurance and property taxes. When the borrower fails to advance these funds, the servicer is typically required to make these payments on behalf of the investor. However, limited effort on the part of the mortgagor to maintain the property has no resolution, and creates incentives for quick foreclosure.
  5) Frictions between the servicer and third-parties: Moral hazard [2.1.5]
     - The income of the servicer is increasing in the amount of time that the loan is serviced. Thus the servicer would prefer to keep the loan on its books for as long as

possible and therefore has a strong preference to modify the terms of a delinquent loan and to delay foreclosure.
- ➢ In the event of delinquency, the servicer has a natural incentive to inflate expenses for which it is reimbursed by the investors, especially in good times when recovery rates on foreclosed property are high.
- ➢ Resolution: servicer quality ratings and a master servicer. Moody's estimates that servicer quality can affect the realized level of losses by plus or minus 10 percent. The master servicer is responsible for monitoring the performance of the servicer under the pooling and servicing agreement.

6) Frictions between the asset manager and investor: Principal-agent [2.1.6]
- ➢ The investor provides the funding for the MBS purchase but is typically not financially sophisticated enough to formulate an investment strategy, conduct due diligence on potential investments, and find the best price for trades. This service is provided by an asset manager (agent) who may not invest sufficient effort on behalf of the investor (principal).
- ➢ Resolution: investment mandates and the evaluation of manager performance relative to a peer group or benchmark

7) Frictions between the investor and the credit rating agencies: Model error [2.1.7]
- ➢ The rating agencies are paid by the arranger and not investors for their opinion, which creates a potential conflict of interest. The opinion is arrived at in part through the use of models (about which the rating agency naturally knows more than the investor) which are susceptible to both honest and dishonest errors.
- ➢ Resolution: the reputation of the rating agencies and the public disclosure of ratings and downgrade criteria.

- Five frictions caused the subprime crisis [2.2]
  - Friction #1: Many products offered to sub-prime borrowers are very complex and subject to mis-understanding and/or mis-representation.
  - Friction #6: Existing investment mandates do not adequately distinguish between structured and corporate ratings. Asset managers had an incentive to reach for yield by purchasing structured debt issues with the same credit rating but higher coupons as corporate debt issues.[1]
  - Friction #3: Without due diligence of the asset manager, the arranger's incentives to conduct its own due diligence are reduced. Moreover, as the market for credit derivatives developed, including but not limited to the ABX, the arranger was able to limit its funded exposure to securitizations of risky loans.
  - Friction #2: Together, frictions 1, 2 and 6 worsened the friction between the originator and arranger, opening the door for predatory borrowing and lending.
  - Friction #7: Credit ratings were assigned to subprime MBS with significant error. Even though the rating agencies publicly disclosed their rating criteria for subprime, investors lacked the ability to evaluate the efficacy of these models.
  - We suggest some improvements to the existing process, though it is not clear that any additional regulation is warranted as the market is already taking remedial steps in the right direction.

---

[1] The fact that the market demands a higher yield for similarly rated structured products than for straight corporate bonds ought to provide a clue to the potential of higher risk.

- An overview of subprime mortgage credit [3] and subprime MBS [4]
- Credit rating agencies (CRAs) play an important role by helping to resolve many of the frictions in the securitization process
    - A credit rating by a CRA represents an overall assessment and opinion of a debt obligor's creditworthiness and is thus meant to reflect only credit or default risk. It is meant to be directly comparable across countries and instruments. Credit ratings typically represent an unconditional view, sometimes called "cycle-neutral" or "through-the-cycle." [5.1]
    - Especially for investment grade ratings, it is very difficult to tell the difference between a "bad" credit rating and bad luck [5.3]
    - The subprime credit rating process can be split into two steps: (1) estimation of a loss distribution, and (2) simulation of the cash flows. With a loss distribution in hand, it is straightforward to measure the amount of credit enhancement necessary for a tranche to attain a given credit rating. [5.4]
    - There seem to be substantial differences between corporate and asset backed securities (ABS) credit ratings (an MBS is just a special case of an ABS – the assets are mortgages) [5.5]
        - Corporate bond (obligor) ratings are largely based on firm-specific risk characteristics. Since ABS structures represent claims on cash flows from a *portfolio* of underlying assets, the rating of a structured credit product must take into account systematic risk.
        - ABS ratings refer to the performance of a static pool instead of a dynamic corporation.
        - ABS ratings rely heavily on quantitative models while corporate debt ratings rely heavily on analyst judgment.
        - Unlike corporate credit ratings, ABS ratings rely explicitly on a forecast of (macro)economic conditions.
        - While an ABS credit rating for a particular rating grade should have similar expected loss to corporate credit rating of the same grade, the volatility of loss (i.e. the *un*expected loss) can be quite different across asset classes.
        - Rating agency must respond to shifts in the loss distribution by increasing the amount of needed credit enhancement to keep ratings stable as economic conditions deteriorate. It follows that the stabilizing of ratings through the cycle is associated with pro-cyclical credit enhancement: as the housing market improves, credit enhancement falls; as the housing market slows down, credit enhancement increases which has the potential to amplify the housing cycle. [5.6]
        - An important part of the rating process involves simulating the cash flows of the structure in order to determine how much credit excess spread will receive towards meeting the required credit enhancement. This is very complicated, with results that can be rather sensitive to underlying model assumptions. [5.7]

Table of Contents

1. Introduction 1
2. Overview of subprime mortgage credit securitization 2
2.1. The seven key frictions 3
2.1.1. Frictions between the mortgagor and originator: Predatory lending 5
2.1.2. Frictions between the originator and the arranger: Predatory lending and borrowing ... 5
2.1.3. Frictions between the arranger and third-parties: Adverse selection 6
2.1.4. Frictions between the servicer and the mortgagor: Moral hazard 7
2.1.5. Frictions between the servicer and third-parties: Moral hazard 8
2.1.6. Frictions between the asset manager and investor: Principal-agent 9
2.1.7. Frictions between the investor and the credit rating agencies: Model error .. 10
2.2. Five frictions that caused the subprime crisis 11
3. An overview of subprime mortgage credit 13
3.1. Who is the subprime mortgagor? 14
3.2. What is a subprime loan? 16
3.3. How have subprime loans performed? 23
3.4. How are subprime loans valued? 26
4. Overview of subprime MBS 29
4.1. Subordination 29
4.2. Excess spread 31
4.3. Shifting interest 32
4.4. Performance triggers 32
4.5. Interest rate swap 33
5. An overview of subprime MBS ratings 36
5.1. What is a credit rating? 37
5.2. How does one become a rating agency? 38
5.3. When is a credit rating wrong? How could we tell? 39
5.4. The subprime credit rating process 40
5.4.1. Credit enhancement 41
5.5. Conceptual differences between corporate and ABS credit ratings 43
5.6. How through-the-cycle rating could amplify the housing cycle 45
5.7. Cash Flow Analytics for Excess Spread 47
5.8. Performance Monitoring 55
5.9. Home Equity ABS rating performance 58
6. The reliance of investors on credit ratings: A case study 61
6.1. Overview of the fund 62
6.2. Fixed-income asset management 64
7. Conclusions 66
References 67
Appendix 1: Predatory Lending 70
Appendix 2: Predatory Borrowing: 72
Appendix 3: Some Estimates of PD by Rating 75

1. Introduction

How does one securitize a pool of mortgages, especially subprime mortgages? What is the process from origination of the loan or mortgage to the selling of debt instruments backed by a pool of those mortgages? What problems creep up in this process, and what are the mechanisms in place to mitigate those problems? This paper seeks to answer all of these questions. Along the way we provide an overview of the market and some of the key players, and provide an extensive discussion of the important role played by the credit rating agencies.

In Section 2, we provide a broad description of the securitization process and pay special attention to seven key frictions that need to be resolved. Several of these frictions involve moral hazard, adverse selection and principal-agent problems. We show how each of these frictions is worked out, though as evidenced by the recent problems in the subprime mortgage market, some of those solutions are imperfect. In Section 3, we provide an overview of subprime mortgage credit; our focus here is on the subprime borrower and the subprime loan. We offer, as an example a pool of subprime mortgages New Century securitized in June 2006. We discuss how predatory lending and predatory borrowing (i.e. mortgage fraud) fit into the picture. Moreover, we examine subprime loan performance within this pool and the industry, speculate on the impact of payment reset, and explore the ABX and the role it plays. In Section 4, we examine subprime mortgage-backed securities, discuss the key structural features of a typical securitization, and, once again illustrate how this works with reference to the New Century securitization. We finish with an examination of the credit rating and rating monitoring process in Section 5. Along the way we reflect on differences between corporate and structured credit ratings, the potential for pro-cyclical credit enhancement to amplify the housing cycle, and document the performance of subprime ratings. Finally, in Section 6, we review the extent to which investors rely upon on credit rating agencies views, and take as a typical example of an investor: the Ohio Police & Fire Pension Fund.

We reiterate that the views presented here are our own and not those of the Federal Reserve Bank of New York or the Federal Reserve System. And, while the paper focuses on subprime mortgage credit, note that there is little qualitative difference between the securitization and ratings process for Alt-A and home equity loans. Clearly, recent problems in mortgage markets are not confined to the subprime sector.

2. Overview of subprime mortgage credit securitization

Until very recently, the origination of mortgages and issuance of mortgage-backed securities (MBS) was dominated by loans to prime borrowers conforming to underwriting standards set by the Government Sponsored Agencies (GSEs). Outside of conforming loans are non-agency asset classes that include Jumbo, Alt-A, and Subprime. Loosely speaking, the Jumbo asset class includes loans to prime borrowers with an original principal balance larger than the conforming limits imposed on the agencies by Congress;[2] the Alt-A asset class involves loans to borrowers with good credit but include more aggressive underwriting than the conforming or Jumbo classes (i.e. no documentation of income, high leverage); and the Subprime asset class involves loans to borrowers with poor credit history.

Table 1 documents origination and issuance since 2001 in each of four asset classes. In 2001, banks originated $1.433 trillion in conforming mortgage loans and issued $1.087 trillion in mortgage-backed securities secured by those mortgages, shown in the "Agency" columns of Table 1. In contrast, the non-agency sector originated $680 billion ($190 billion subprime + $60 billion Alt-A + $430 billion jumbo) and issued $240 billion ($87.1 billion subprime + $11.4 Alt-A + $142.2 billion jumbo), and most of these were in the Jumbo sector. The Alt-A and Subprime sectors were relatively small, together comprising $250 billion of $2.1 trillion (12 percent) in total origination during 2001.

Table 1: Origination and Issue of Non-Agency Mortgage Loans

	Sub-prime			Alt-A			Jumbo			Agency		
Year	Origination	Issuance	Ratio	Origination	Issuance	Ratio	Origination	Issuance	Ratio	Origination	Issuance	Ratio
2001	$ 190.00	$ 87.10	46%	$ 60.00	$ 11.40	19%	$ 430.00	$ 142.20	33%	$ 1,433.00	$1,087.60	76%
2002	$ 231.00	$ 122.70	53%	$ 68.00	$ 53.50	79%	$ 576.00	$ 171.50	30%	$ 1,898.00	$1,442.60	76%
2003	$ 335.00	$ 195.00	58%	$ 85.00	$ 74.10	87%	$ 655.00	$ 237.50	36%	$ 2,690.00	$2,130.90	79%
2004	$ 540.00	$ 362.63	67%	$ 200.00	$ 158.60	79%	$ 515.00	$ 233.40	45%	$ 1,345.00	$1,018.60	76%
2005	$ 625.00	$ 465.00	74%	$ 380.00	$ 332.30	87%	$ 570.00	$ 280.70	49%	$ 1,180.00	$ 964.80	82%
2006	$ 600.00	$ 448.60	75%	$ 400.00	$ 365.70	91%	$ 480.00	$ 219.00	46%	$ 1,040.00	$ 904.60	87%

Source: Inside Mortgage Finance (2007).
Notes: Jumbo origination includes non-agency prime. Agency origination includes conventional/conforming and FHA/VA loans. Agency issuance GNMA, FHLMC, and FNMA. Figures are in billions of USD.

A reduction in long-term interest rates through the end of 2003 was associated with a sharp increase in origination and issuance across all asset classes. While the conforming markets peaked in 2003, the non-agency markets continued rapid growth through 2005, eventually eclipsing activity in the conforming market. In 2006, non-agency production of $1.480 trillion was more than 45 percent larger than agency production, and non-agency issuance of $1.033 trillion was larger than agency issuance of $905 billion.

Interestingly, the increase in Subprime and Alt-A origination was associated with a significant increase in the ratio of issuance to origination, which is a reasonable proxy for the fraction of loans sold. In particular, the ratio of subprime MBS issuance to subprime mortgage origination was close to 75 percent in both 2005 and 2006. While there is typically a one-quarter lag between origination and issuance, the data document that a large and increasing fraction of both subprime and Alt-A loans are sold to investors, and very little is retained on the balance sheets of the institutions who originate them. The process through which loans are removed from the

---

[2] This limit is currently $417,000.

balance sheet of lenders and transformed into debt securities purchased by investors is called securitization.

2.1. The seven key frictions

The securitization of mortgage loans is a complex process that involves a number of different players. Figure 1 provides an overview of the players, their responsibilities, the important frictions that exist between the players, and the mechanisms used in order to mitigate these frictions. An overarching friction which plagues every step in the process is asymmetric information: usually one party has more information about the asset than another. We think that understanding these frictions and evaluating the mechanisms designed to mitigate their importance is essential to understanding how the securitization of subprime loans could generate bad outcomes.[3]

Figure 1: Key Players and Frictions in Subprime Mortgage Credit Securitization

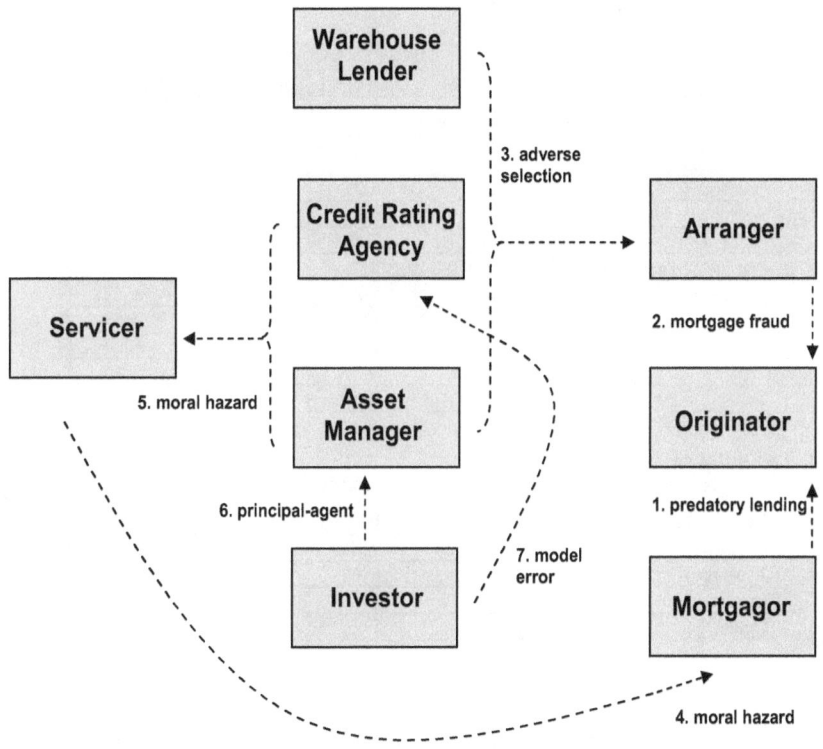

---

[3] A recent piece in *The Economist* (September 20, 2007) provides a nice description of some of the frictions described here.

Table 2: Top Subprime Mortgage Originators

		2006		2005	
Rank	Lender	Volume ($b)	Share (%)	Volume ($b)	%Change
1	HSBC	$52.8	8.8%	$58.6	-9.9%
2	New Century Financial	$51.6	8.6%	$52.7	-2.1%
3	Countrywide	$40.6	6.8%	$44.6	-9.1%
4	CitiGroup	$38.0	6.3%	$20.5	85.5%
5	WMC Mortgage	$33.2	5.5%	$31.8	4.3%
6	Fremont	$32.3	5.4%	$36.2	-10.9%
7	Ameriquest Mortgage	$29.5	4.9%	$75.6	-61.0%
8	Option One	$28.8	4.8%	$40.3	-28.6%
9	Wells Fargo	$27.9	4.6%	$30.3	-8.1%
10	First Franklin	$27.7	4.6%	$29.3	-5.7%
	Top 25	$543.2	90.5%	$604.9	-10.2%
	Total	$600.0	100.0%	$664.0	-9.8%

Source: Inside Mortgage Finance (2007)

Table 3: Top Subprime MBS Issuers

		2006		2005	
Rank	Lender	Volume ($b)	Share (%)	Volume ($b)	%Change
1	Countrywide	$38.5	8.6%	$38.1	1.1%
2	New Century	$33.9	7.6%	$32.4	4.8%
3	Option One	$31.3	7.0%	$27.2	15.1%
4	Fremont	$29.8	6.6%	$19.4	53.9%
5	Washington Mutual	$28.8	6.4%	$18.5	65.1%
6	First Franklin	$28.3	6.3%	$19.4	45.7%
7	Residential Funding Corp	$25.9	5.8%	$28.7	-9.5%
8	Lehman Brothers	$24.4	5.4%	$35.3	-30.7%
9	WMC Mortgage	$21.6	4.8%	$19.6	10.5%
10	Ameriquest	$21.4	4.8%	$54.2	-60.5%
	Top 25	$427.6	95.3%	$417.6	2.4%
	Total	$448.6	100.0%	$508.0	-11.7%

Source: Inside Mortgage Finance (2007)

Table 4: Top Subprime Mortgage Servicers

		2006		2005	
Rank	Lender	Volume ($b)	Share (%)	Volume ($b)	%Change
1	Countrywide	$119.1	9.6%	$120.6	-1.3%
2	JP MorganChase	$83.8	6.8%	$67.8	23.6%
3	CitiGroup	$80.1	6.5%	$47.3	39.8%
4	Option One	$69.0	5.6%	$79.5	-13.2%
5	Ameriquest	$60.0	4.8%	$75.4	-20.4%
6	Ocwen Financial Corp	$52.2	4.2%	$42.0	24.2%
7	Wells Fargo	$51.3	4.1%	$44.7	14.8%
8	Homecomings Financial	$49.5	4.0%	$55.2	-10.4%
9	HSBC	$49..5	4.0%	$43.8	13.0%
10	Litton Loan Servicing	$47.0	4.0%	$42.0	16.7%
	Top 30	$1,105.7	89.2%	$1,057.8	4.5%
	Total	$1,240	100.0%	$1,200	3.3%

Source: Inside Mortgage Finance (2007)

2.1.1. Frictions between the mortgagor and originator: Predatory lending

The process starts with the mortgagor or borrower, who applies for a mortgage in order to purchase a property or to refinance and existing mortgage. The originator, possibly through a broker (yet another intermediary in this process), underwrites and initially funds and services the mortgage loans. Table 2 documents the top 10 subprime originators in 2006, which are a healthy mix of commercial banks and non-depository specialized mono-line lenders. The originator is compensated through fees paid by the borrower (points and closing costs), and by the proceeds of the sale of the mortgage loans. For example, the originator might sell a portfolio of loans with an initial principal balance of $100 million for $102 million, corresponding to a gain on sale of $2 million. The buyer is willing to pay this premium because of anticipated interest payments on the principal.

The first friction in securitization is between the borrower and the originator. In particular, subprime borrowers can be financially unsophisticated. For example, a borrower might be unaware of all of the financial options available to him. Moreover, even if these options are known, the borrower might be unable to make a choice between different financial options that is in his own best interest. This friction leads to the possibility of predatory lending, defined by Morgan (2005) as the welfare-reducing provision of credit. The main safeguards against these practices are federal, state, and local laws prohibiting certain lending practices, as well as the recent regulatory guidance on subprime lending. See Appendix 1 for further discussion of these issues.

2.1.2. Frictions between the originator and the arranger: Predatory lending and borrowing

The pool of mortgage loans is typically purchased from the originator by an institution known as the arranger or issuer. The first responsibility of the arranger is to conduct due diligence on the originator. This review includes but is not limited to financial statements, underwriting guidelines, discussions with senior management, and background checks. The arranger is responsible for bringing together all the elements for the deal to close. In particular, the arranger creates a bankruptcy-remote trust that will purchase the mortgage loans, consults with the credit rating agencies in order to finalize the details about deal structure, makes necessary filings with the SEC, and underwrites the issuance of securities by the trust to investors. Table 3 documents the list of the top 10 subprime MBS issuers in 2006. In addition to institutions which both originate and issue on their own, the list of issuers also includes investment banks that purchase mortgages from originators and issue their own securities. The arranger is typically compensated through fees charged to investors and through any premium that investors pay on the issued securities over their par value.

The second friction in the process of securitization involves an information problem between the originator and arranger. In particular, the originator has an information advantage over the arranger with regard to the quality of the borrower. Without adequate safeguards in place, an originator can have the incentive to collaborate with a borrower in order to make significant misrepresentations on the loan application, which, depending on the situation, could be either construed as predatory lending (the lender convinces the borrower to borrow "too much") or predatory borrowing (the borrower convinces the lender to lend "too much"). See Appendix 2 on predatory borrowing for further discussion.

There are several important checks designed to prevent mortgage fraud, the first being the due diligence of the arranger. In addition, the originator typically makes a number of representations and warranties (R&W) about the borrower and the underwriting process. When these are violated, the originator generally must repurchase the problem loans. However, in order for these promises to have a meaningful impact on the friction, the originator must have adequate capital to buy back those problem loans. Moreover, when an arranger does not conduct or routinely ignores its own due diligence, as suggested in a recent Reuters piece by Rucker (1 Aug 2007), there is little to stop the originator from committing widespread mortgage fraud.

2.1.3. Frictions between the arranger and third-parties: Adverse selection

There is an important information asymmetry between the arranger and third-parties concerning the quality of mortgage loans. In particular, the fact that the arranger has more information about the quality of the mortgage loans creates an adverse selection problem: the arranger can securitize bad loans (the lemons) and keep the good ones (or securitize them elsewhere). This third friction in the securitization of subprime loans affects the relationship that the arranger has with the warehouse lender, the credit rating agency (CRA), and the asset manager. We discuss how each of these parties responds to this classic lemons problem.

Adverse selection and the warehouse lender

The arranger is responsible for funding the mortgage loans until all of the details of the securitization deal can be finalized. When the arranger is a depository institution, this can be done easily with internal funds. However, mono-line arrangers typically require funding from a third-party lender for loans kept in the "warehouse" until they can be sold. Since the lender is uncertain about the value of the mortgage loans, it must take steps to protect itself against overvaluing their worth as collateral. This is accomplished through due diligence by the lender, haircuts to the value of collateral, and credit spreads. The use of haircuts to the value of collateral imply that the bank loan is over-collateralized (o/c) – it might extend a $9 million loan against collateral of $10 million of underlying mortgages –, forcing the arranger to assume a funded equity position – in this case $1 million – in the loans while they remain on its balance sheet.

We emphasize this friction because an adverse change in the warehouse lender's views of the value of the underlying loans can bring an originator to its knees. The failure of dozens of mono-line originators in the first half of 2007 can be explained in large part by the inability of these firms to respond to increased demands for collateral by warehouse lenders (Wei, 2007; Sichelman, 2007).

Adverse selection and the asset manager

The pool of mortgage loans is sold by the arranger to a bankruptcy-remote trust, which is a special-purpose vehicle that issues debt to investors. This trust is an essential component of credit risk transfer, as it protects investors from bankruptcy of the originator or arranger. Moreover, the sale of loans to the trust protects both the originator and arranger from losses on the mortgage loans, provided that there have been no breaches of representations and warranties made by the originator.

The arranger underwrites the sale of securities secured by the pool of subprime mortgage loans to an asset manager, who is an agent for the ultimate investor. However, the information advantage of the arranger creates a standard lemons problem. This problem is mitigated by the market through the following means: reputation of the arranger, the arranger providing a credit enhancement to the securities with its own funding, and any due diligence conducted by the portfolio manager on the arranger and originator.

Adverse selection and credit rating agencies

The rating agencies assign credit ratings on mortgage-backed securities issued by the trust. These opinions about credit quality are determined using publicly available rating criteria which map the characteristics of the pool of mortgage loans into an estimated loss distribution. From this loss distribution, the rating agencies calculate the amount of credit enhancement that a security requires in order for it to attain a given credit rating. The opinion of the rating agencies is vulnerable to the lemons problem (the arranger likely still knows more) because they only conduct limited due diligence on the arranger and originator.

2.1.4. Frictions between the servicer and the mortgagor: Moral hazard

The trust employs a servicer who is responsible for collection and remittance of loan payments, making advances of unpaid interest by borrowers to the trust, accounting for principal and interest, customer service to the mortgagors, holding escrow or impounding funds related to payment of taxes and insurance, contacting delinquent borrowers, and supervising foreclosures and property dispositions. The servicer is compensated through a periodic fee by paid the trust. Table 4 documents the top 10 subprime servicers in 2006, which is a mix of depository institutions and specialty non-depository mono-line servicing companies.

Moral hazard refers to changes in behavior in response to redistribution of risk, e.g., insurance may induce risk-taking behavior if the insured does not bear the full consequences of bad outcomes. Here we have a problem where one party (the mortgagor) has unobserved costly effort that affects the distribution over cash flows which are shared with another party (the servicer), and the first party has limited liability (it does not share in downside risk). In managing delinquent loans, the servicer is faced with a standard moral hazard problem vis-à-vis the mortgagor. When a servicer has the incentive to work in investors' best interest, it will manage delinquent loans in a fashion to minimize losses. A mortgagor struggling to make a mortgage payment is also likely struggling to keep hazard insurance and property tax bills current, as well as conduct adequate maintenance on the property. The failure to pay property taxes could result in costly liens on the property that increase the costs to investors of ultimately foreclosing on the property. The failure to pay hazard insurance premiums could result in a lapse in coverage, exposing investors to the risk of significant loss. And the failure to maintain the property will increase expenses to investors in marketing the property after foreclosure and possibly reduce the sale price. The mortgagor has little incentive to expend effort or resources to maintain a property close to foreclosure.

In order to prevent these potential problems from surfacing, it is standard practice to require the mortgagor to regularly escrow funds for both insurance and property taxes. When the borrower fails to advance these funds, the servicer is typically required to make these payments on behalf of the investor. In order to prevent lapses in maintenance from creating losses, the servicer is encouraged to foreclose promptly on the property once it is deemed uncollectible. An important constraint in resolving this latter issue is that the ability of a servicer to collect on a delinquent debt is generally restricted under the Real Estate Settlement Procedures Act, Fair Debt Collection Practices Act and state deceptive trade practices statutes. In a recent court case, a plaintiff in Texas alleging unlawful collection activities against Ocwen Financial was awarded $12.5 million in actual and punitive damages.

2.1.5. Frictions between the servicer and third-parties: Moral hazard

The servicer can have a significantly positive or negative effect on the losses realized from the mortgage pool. Moody's estimates that servicer quality can affect the realized level of losses by plus or minus 10 percent. This impact of servicer quality on losses has important implications for both investors and credit rating agencies. In particular, investors want to minimize losses while credit rating agencies want to minimize the uncertainty about losses in order to make accurate opinions. In each case articulated below we have a similar problem as in the fourth friction, namely where one party (here the servicer) has unobserved costly effort that affects the distribution over cash flows which are shared with other parties, and the first party has limited liability (it does not share in downside risk).

Moral hazard between the servicer and the asset manager[4]

The servicing fee is a flat percentage of the outstanding principal balance of mortgage loans. The servicer is paid first out of receipts each month before any funds are advanced to investors. Since mortgage payments are generally received at the beginning of the month and investors receive their distributions near the end of the month, the servicer benefits from being able to earn interest on float.[5]

There are two key points of tension between investors and the servicer: (a) reasonable reimbursable expenses, and (b) the decision to modify and foreclose. We discuss each of these in turn.

In the event of a delinquency, the servicer must advance unpaid interest (and sometimes principal) to the trust as long as it is deemed collectable, which typically means that the loan is less than 90 days delinquent. In addition to advancing unpaid interest, the servicer must also keep paying property taxes and insurance premiums as long as it has a mortgage on the property. In the event of foreclosure, the servicer must pay all expenses out of pocket until the property is liquidated, at which point it is reimbursed for advances and expenses. The servicer has a natural incentive to inflate expenses, especially in good times when recovery rates on foreclosed property are high.

---

[4] Several points raised in this section were first raised in a 20 February 2007 post on the blog http://calculatedrisk.blogspot.com/ entitled "Mortgage Servicing for Ubernerds."
[5] In addition to the monthly fee, the servicer generally gets to keep late fees. This can tempt a servicer to post payments in a tardy fashion or not make collection calls until late fees are assessed.

Note that the un-reimbursable expenses of the servicer are largely fixed and front-loaded: registering the loan in the servicing system, getting the initial notices out, doing the initial escrow analysis and tax setups, etc. At the same time, the income of the servicer is increasing in the amount of time that the loan is serviced. It follows that the servicer would prefer to keep the loan on its books for as long as possible. This means it has a strong preference to modify the terms of a delinquent loan and to delay foreclosure.

Resolving each of these problems involves a delicate balance. On the one hand, one can put hard rules into the pooling and servicing agreement limiting loan modifications, and an investor can invest effort into actively monitoring the servicer's expenses. On the other hand, the investor wants to give the servicer flexibility to act in the investor's best interest and does not want to incur too much expense in monitoring. This latter point is especially true since other investors will free-ride off of any one investor's effort. It is not surprising that the credit rating agencies play an important role in resolving this collective action problem through servicer quality ratings.

In addition to monitoring effort by investors, servicer quality ratings, and rules about loan modifications, there are two other important ways to mitigate this friction: servicer reputation and the master servicer. As the servicing business is an important counter-cyclical source of income for banks, one would think that these institutions would work hard on their own to minimize this friction. The master servicer is responsible for monitoring the performance of the servicer under the pooling and servicing agreement. It validates data reported by the servicer, reviews the servicing of defaulted loans, and enforces remedies of servicer default on behalf of the trust.

Moral hazard between the servicer and the credit rating agency

Given the impact of servicer quality on losses, the accuracy of the credit rating placed on securities issued by the trust is vulnerable to the use of a low quality servicer. In order to minimize the impact of this friction, the rating agencies conduct due diligence on the servicer, use the results of this analysis in the rating of mortgage-backed securities, and release their findings to the public for use by investors.

Servicer quality ratings are intended to be an unbiased benchmark of a loan servicer's ability to prevent or mitigate pool losses across changing market conditions. This evaluation includes an assessment of collections/customer service, loss mitigation, foreclosure timeline management, management, staffing & training, financial stability, technology and disaster recovery, legal compliance and oversight and financial strength. In constructing these quality ratings, the rating agency attempts to break out the actual historical loss experience of the servicer into an amount attributable to the underlying credit risk of the loans and an amount attributable to the servicer's collection and default management ability.

2.1.6. Frictions between the asset manager and investor: Principal-agent

The investor provides the funding for the purchase of the mortgage-backed security. As the investor is typically financially unsophisticated, an agent is employed to formulate an investment strategy, conduct due diligence on potential investments, and find the best price for trades. Given differences in the degree of financial sophistication between the investor and an asset manager, there is an obvious information problem between the investor and portfolio manger that gives rise to the sixth friction.

In particular, the investor will not fully understand the investment strategy of the manager, has uncertainty about the manager's ability, and does not observe any effort that the manager makes to conduct due diligence. This principal (investor)-agent (manager) problem is mitigated through the use of investment mandates, and the evaluation of manager performance relative to a peer benchmark or its peers.

As one example, a public pension might restrict the investments of an asset manager to debt securities with an investment grade credit rating and evaluate the performance of an asset manager relative to a benchmark index. However, there are other relevant examples. The FDIC, which is an implicit investor in commercial banks through the provision of deposit insurance, prevents insured banks from investing in speculative-grade securities or enforces risk-based capital requirements that use credit ratings to assess risk-weights. An actively-managed collateralized debt obligation (CDO) imposes covenants on the weighted average rating of securities in an actively-managed portfolio as well as the fraction of securities with a low credit rating.

As investment mandates typically involve credit ratings, it should be clear that this is another point where the credit rating agencies play an important role in the securitization process. By presenting an opinion on the riskiness of offered securities, the rating agencies help resolve the information frictions that exist between the investor and the portfolio manager. Credit ratings are intended to capture the expectations about the long-run or through-the-cycle performance of a debt security. A credit rating is fundamentally a statement about the suitability of an instrument to be included in a risk class, but importantly, it is an opinion only about credit risk; we discuss credit ratings in more detail in Section 5.1. It follows that the opinion of credit rating agencies is a crucial part of securitization, because in the end the rating is the means through which much of the funding by investors finds its way into the deal.

2.1.7. Frictions between the investor and the credit rating agencies: Model error

The rating agencies are paid by the arranger and not investors for their opinion, which creates a potential conflict of interest. Since an investor is not able to assess the efficacy of rating agency models, they are susceptible to both honest and dishonest errors on the agencies' part. The information asymmetry between investors and the credit rating agencies is the seventh and final friction in the securitization process. Honest errors are a natural byproduct of rapid financial innovation and complexity. On the other hand, dishonest errors could be driven by the dependence of rating agencies on fees paid by the arranger (the conflict of interest).

Some critics claim that the rating agencies are unable to objectively rate structured products due to conflicts of interest created by issuer-paid fees. Moody's, for example, made 44 per cent of its revenue last year from structured finance deals (Tomlinson and Evans, 2007). Such assessments also command more than double the fee rates of simpler corporate ratings, helping keep Moody's operating margins above 50 per cent (Economist, 2007).

Beales, Scholtes and Tett (15 May 2007) write in the *Financial Times*:

The potential for conflicts of interest in the agencies' "issuer pays" model has drawn fire before, but the scale of their dependence on investment banks for structured finance business gives them a significant incentive to look kindly on the products they are rating, critics say. From his office in Paris, the head of the Autorité des Marchés Financiers, the main French financial regulator, is raising fresh questions over their role and objectivity. Mr Prada sees the possibility for conflicts of interest similar to those that emerged in the audit profession when it drifted into consulting. Here, the integrity of the auditing work was threatened by the demands of winning and retaining clients in the more lucrative consultancy business, a conflict that ultimately helped bring down accountants Arthur Andersen in the wake of Enron's collapse. "I do hope that it does not take another Enron for everyone to look at the issue of rating agencies," he says.

This friction is minimized through two devices: the reputation of the rating agencies and the public disclosure of ratings and downgrade criteria. For the rating agencies, their business is their reputation, so it is difficult – though not impossible – to imagine that they would risk deliberately inflating credit ratings in order to earn structuring fees, thus jeopardizing their franchise. Moreover, with public rating and downgrade criteria, any deviations in credit ratings from their models are easily observed by the public.[6]

2.2. Five frictions that caused the subprime crisis

We believe that five of the seven frictions discussed above help to explain the breakdown in the subprime mortgage market.

The problem starts with friction #1: many products offered to sub-prime borrowers are very complex and subject to mis-understanding and/or mis-representation. This opened the possibility of both excessive borrowing (predatory borrowing) and excessive lending (predatory lending).

At the other end of the process we have the principal-agent problem between the investor and asset manager (friction #6). In particular, it seems that investment mandates do not adequately distinguish between structured and corporate credit ratings. This is a problem because asset manager performance is evaluated relative to peers or relative to a benchmark index. It follows that asset managers have an incentive to reach for yield by purchasing structured debt issues with the same credit rating but higher coupons as corporate debt issues.[7]

Initially, this portfolio shift was likely led by asset managers with the ability to conduct their own due diligence, recognizing value in the wide pricing of subprime mortgage-backed securities. However, once the other asset managers started to under-perform their peers, they likely made similar portfolio shifts, but did not invest the same effort into due diligence of the arranger and originator.

This phenomenon worsened the friction between the arranger and the asset manager (friction #3). In particular, without due diligence by the asset manager, the arranger's incentives to conduct its own due diligence are reduced. Moreover, as the market for credit derivatives

---

[6] We think that there are two ways these errors could emerge. One, the rating agency builds its model honestly, but then applies judgment in a fashion consistent with its economic interest. The average deal is structured appropriately, but the agency gives certain issuers better terms. Two, the model itself is knowingly aggressive. The average deal is structured inadequately.

[7] The fact that the market demands a higher yield for similarly rated structured products than for straight corporate bonds ought to provide a clue to the potential of higher risk.

developed, including but not limited to the ABX, the arranger was able to limit its funded exposure to securitizations of risky loans. Together, these considerations worsened the friction between the originator and arranger, opening the door for predatory borrowing and provides incentives for predatory lending (friction #2). In the end, the only constraint on underwriting standards was the opinion of the rating agencies. With limited capital backing representations and warranties, an originator could easily arbitrage rating agency models, exploiting the weak historical relationship between aggressive underwriting and losses in the data used to calibrate required credit enhancement.

The inability of the rating agencies to recognize this arbitrage by originators and respond appropriately meant that credit ratings were assigned to subprime mortgage-backed securities with significant error. The friction between investors and the rating agencies is the final nail in the coffin (friction #7). Even though the rating agencies publicly disclosed their rating criteria for subprime, investors lacked the ability to evaluate the efficacy of these models.

While we have identified seven frictions in the mortgage securitization process, there are mechanisms in place to mitigate or even resolve each of these frictions, including for example anti-predatory lending laws and regulations. As we have seen, some of these mechanisms have failed to deliver as promised. Is it hard to fix this process? We believe not, and we think the solution might start with investment mandates. Investors should realize the incentives of asset managers to push for yield. Investments in structured products should be compared to a benchmark index of investments in the same asset class. When investors or asset managers are forced to conduct their own due diligence in order to outperform the index, the incentives of the arranger and originator are restored. Moreover, investors should demand that either the arranger or originator – or even both – retain the first-loss or equity tranche of every securitization, and disclose all hedges of this position. At the end of the production chain, originators need to be adequately capitalized so that their representations and warranties have value. Finally, the rating agencies could evaluate originators with the same rigor that they evaluate servicers, including perhaps the designation of originator ratings.

It is not clear to us that any of these solutions require additional regulation, and note that the market is already taking steps in the right direction. For example, the credit rating agencies have already responded with greater transparency and have announced significant changes in the rating process. In addition, the demand for structured credit products generally and subprime mortgage securitizations in particular has declined significantly as investors have started to re-assess their own views of the risk in these products. Along these lines, it may be advisable for policymakers to give the market a chance to self-correct.

3. An overview of subprime mortgage credit

In this section, we shed some light on the subprime mortgagor, work through the details of a typical subprime mortgage loan, and review the historical performance of subprime mortgage credit.

The motivating example

In order to keep the discussion from becoming too abstract, we find it useful to frame many of these issues in the context of a real-life example which will be used throughout the paper. In particular, we focus on a securitization of 3,949 subprime loans with aggregate principal balance of $881 million originated by New Century Financial in the second quarter of 2006.[8]

Our view is that this particular securitization is interesting because illustrates how typical subprime loans from what proved to be the worst-performing vintage came to be originated, structured, and ultimately sold to investors. In each of the years 2004 to 2006, New Century Financial was the second largest subprime lender, originating $51.6 billion in mortgage loans during 2006 (Inside Mortgage Finance, 2007). Volume grew at a compound annual growth rate of 59% between 2000 and 2004. The backbone of this growth was an automated internet-based loan submission and pre-approval system called *FastQual*. The performance of New Century loans closely tracked that of the industry through the 2005 vintage (Moody's, 2005b). However, the company struggled with early payment defaults in early 2007, failed to meet a call for more collateral on its warehouse lines of credit on 2 March 2007 and ultimately filed for bankruptcy protection on 2 April 2007. The junior tranches of this securitization were part of the historical downgrade action by the rating agencies during the week of 9 July 2007 that affected almost half of first-lien home equity ABS deals issued in 2006.

As illustrated in Figure 2, these loans were initially purchased by a subsidiary of Goldman Sachs, who in turn sold the loans to a bankruptcy-remote special purpose vehicle named GSAMP TRUST 2006-NC2. The trust funded the purchase of these loans through the issue of asset-backed securities, which required the filing of a prospectus with the SEC detailing the transaction. New Century serviced the loans initially, but upon creation of the trust, this business was transferred to Ocwen Loan Servicing, LLC in August 2006, who receives a fee of 50 basis points (or $4.4 million) per year on a monthly basis. The master servicer and securities administrator is Wells Fargo, who receives a fee of 1 basis point (or $881K) per year on a monthly basis. The prospectus includes a list of 26 reps and warranties made by the originator. Some of the items include: the absence of any delinquencies or defaults in the pool; compliance of the mortgages with federal, state, and local laws; the presence of title and hazard insurance; disclosure of fees and points to the borrower; statement that the lender did not encourage or require the borrower to select a higher cost loan product intended for less creditworthy borrowers when they qualified for a more standard loan product.

---

[8] The details of this transaction are taken from the prospectus filed with the SEC and with monthly remittance reports filed with the Trustee. The former is available on-line using the Edgar database at http://www.sec.gov/edgar/searchedgar/companysearch.html with the company name GSAMP Trust 2006-NC2 while the latter is available with free registration from http://www.absnet.net/.

Figure 2: Key Institutions Surrounding GSAMP Trust 2006-NC2

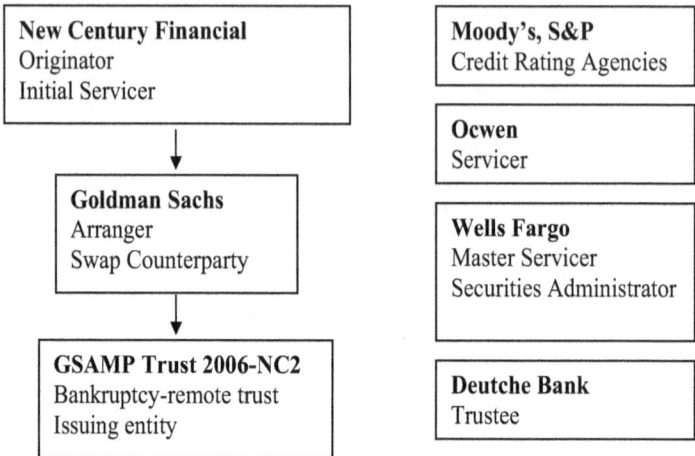

Source: Prospectus filed with the SEC of GSAMP 2006-NC2

3.1. Who is the subprime mortgagor?

The 2001 *Interagency Expanded Guidance for Subprime Lending Programs* defines the subprime borrower as one who generally displays a range of credit risk characteristics, including one or more of the following:

- Two or more 30-day delinquencies in the last 12 months, or one or more 60-day delinquencies in the last 24 months;
- Judgment, foreclosure, repossession, or charge-off in the prior 24 months;
- Bankruptcy in the last 5 years;
- Relatively high default probability as evidenced by, for example, a credit bureau risk score (FICO) of 660 or below (depending on the product/collateral), or other bureau or proprietary scores with an equivalent default probability likelihood; and/or,
- Debt service-to-income ratio of 50 percent or greater; or, otherwise limited ability to cover family living expenses after deducting total debt-service requirements from monthly income.

The motivating example

The pool of mortgage loans used as collateral in the New Century securitization can be summarized as follows:

- 98.7% of the mortgage loans are first-lien. The rest are second-lien home equity loans.

- 43.3% are purchase loans, meaning that the mortgagor's stated purpose for the loan was to purchase a property. The remaining loans' stated purpose are cash-out refinance of existing mortgage loans.
- 90.7% of the mortgagors claim to occupy the property as their primary residence. The remaining mortgagors claim to be investors or purchasing second homes.
- 73.4% of the mortgaged properties are single-family homes. The remaining properties are split between multi-family dwellings or condos.
- 38.0% and 10.5% are secured by residences in California and Florida, respectively, the two dominant states in this securitization.
- The average borrower in the pool has a FICO score of 626. Note that 31.4% have a FICO score below 600, 51.9% between 600 and 660, and 16.7% above 660.
- The combined loan-to value ratio is sum of the original principal balance of all loans secured by the property to its appraised value. The average mortgage loan in the pool has a CLTV of 80.34%. However, 62.1% have a CLTV of 80% or lower, 28.6% between 80% and 90%, and 9.3% between 90% and 100%.
- The ratio of total debt service of the borrower (including the mortgage, property taxes and insurance, and other monthly debt payments) to gross income (income before taxes) is 41.78%.

It is worth pausing here to make a few observations. First, the stated purpose of the majority of these loans is not to purchase a home, but rather to refinance an existing mortgage loan. Second, 90 percent of the borrowers in this portfolio have at least 10 percent equity in their homes. Third, while it might be surprising to find borrowers with a FICO score above 660 in the pool, these loans are much more aggressively underwritten than the loans to the lower FICO-score borrowers. In particular, while not reported in the figures above, loans to borrowers with high FICO scores tend to be much larger, have a higher CLTV, are less likely to use full-documentation, and are less likely to be owner-occupied. The combination of good credit with aggressive underwriting suggests that many of these borrowers could be investors looking to take advantage of rapid home price appreciation in order to re-sell houses for profit. Finally, while the average loan size in the pool is $223,221, much of the aggregate principal balance of the pool is made up of large loans. In particular, 24% of the total number of loans are in excess of $300,000 and make up about 45% of the principal balance of the pool.

Industry trends

Table 5 documents average borrower characteristics for loans contained in Alt-A and Subprime MBS pools in panel (a) and (b), respectively, broken out by year of origination. The most dramatic difference between the two panels is the credit score, as the average Alt-A borrower has a FICO score that is 85 points higher than the average Subprime borrower in 2006 (703 versus 623). Subprime borrowers typically have a higher CLTV, but are more likely to document income and are less likely to purchase a home. Alt-A borrowers are more likely to be investors and are more likely to have silent 2nd liens on the property. Together, these summary statistics suggest that the example securitization discussed seems to be representative of the industry, at least with respect to stated borrower characteristics.

The industry data is also useful to better understand trends in the subprime market that one would not observe by focusing on one deal from 2006. In particular, the CLTV of a subprime loan has been increasing since 1999, as has the fraction of loans with silent second liens. A silent second is a second mortgage that was not disclosed to the first mortgage lender at the time of origination. Moreover, the table illustrates that borrowers have become less likely to document their income over time, and that the fraction of borrowers using the loan to purchase a property has increased significantly since the start of the decade. Together, these data suggest that the average subprime borrower has become significantly more risky in the last two years.

Table 5: Underwriting Characteristics of Loans in MBS Pools

	CLTV	Full Doc	Purchase	Investor	No Prepayment Penalty	FICO	Silent 2nd lien
A. Alt-A Loans							
1999	77.5	38.4	51.8	18.6	79.4	696	0.1
2000	80.2	35.4	68.0	13.8	79.0	697	0.2
2001	77.7	34.8	50.4	8.2	78.8	703	1.4
2002	76.5	36.0	47.4	12.5	70.1	708	2.4
2003	74.9	33.0	39.4	18.5	71.2	711	12.4
2004	79.5	32.4	53.9	17.0	64.8	708	28.6
2005	79.0	27.4	49.4	14.8	56.9	713	32.4
2006	80.6	16.4	45.7	12.9	47.9	708	38.9
B. Subprime Loans							
1999	78.8	68.7	30.1	5.3	28.7	605	0.5
2000	79.5	73.4	36.2	5.5	25.4	596	1.3
2001	80.3	71.5	31.3	5.3	21.0	605	2.8
2002	80.7	65.9	29.9	5.4	20.3	614	2.9
2003	82.4	63.9	30.2	5.6	23.2	624	7.3
2004	83.9	62.2	35.7	5.6	24.6	624	15.8
2005	85.3	58.3	40.5	5.5	26.8	627	24.6
2006	85.5	57.7	42.1	5.6	28.9	623	27.5

All entries are in percentage points except FICO.
Source: LoanPerformance (2007)

3.2. What is a subprime loan?

The motivating example

Table 6 documents that only 8.98% of the loans by dollar-value in the New Century pool are traditional 30-year fixed-rate mortgages (FRMs). The pool also includes a small fraction – 2.81% -- of fixed-rate mortgages which amortize over 40 years, but mature in 30 years, and consequently have a balloon payment after 30 years. Note that 88.2% of the mortgage loans by dollar value are adjustable-rate loans (ARMs), and that each of these loans is a variation on the 2/28 and 3/27 hybrid ARM. These loans are known as hybrids because they have both fixed- and adjustable-rate features to them. In particular, the initial monthly payment is based on a "teaser" interest rate that is fixed for the first two (for the 2/28) or three (for the 3/27) years, and is lower than what a borrower would pay for a 30-year fixed rate mortgage (FRM). The table documents that the average initial interest rate for a vanilla 2/28 loan in the first row is 8.64%. However, after this initial period, the monthly payment is based on a higher interest rate, equal to the value of an interest rate index (i.e. 6-month LIBOR) measured at the time of adjustment, plus a margin that is fixed for the life of the loan. Focusing again on the first 2/28, the margin is 6.22% and LIBOR at the time of origination is 5.31%. This interest rate is updated every six months for the life of the loan, and is subject to limits called adjustment caps on the amount that it can increase: the cap on the first adjustment is called the initial cap; the cap on each subsequent adjustment is called the period cap; the cap on the interest rate over the life of the loan is called the lifetime cap; and the floor on the interest rate is called the floor. In our example of a simple 2/28 ARM, these caps are equal to 1.49%, 1.50%, 15.62%, and 8.62% for the average loan. More than half of the dollar value of the loans in this pool are a 2/28 ARM with a 40-year amortization schedule in order to calculate monthly payments. A substantial fraction are a 2/28 ARM with a five-year interest-only option. This loan permits the borrower to only pay interest for the first sixty months of the loan, but then must make payments in order to repay the loan in the final 25 years. While not noted in the table, the prospectus indicates that none of the mortgage loans carry mortgage insurance. Moreover, approximately 72.5% of the loans include prepayment penalties which expire after one to three years.

These ARMs are rather complex financial instruments with payout features often found in interest rate derivatives. In contrast to a FRM, the mortgagor retains most of the interest rate risk, subject to a collar (a floor and a cap). Note that most mortgagors are not in a position to easily hedge away this interest rate risk.

Table 7 illustrates the monthly payment across loan type, using the average terms for each loan type, a principal balance of $225,000, and making the assumption that six-month LIBOR remains constant. The payment for the 30-year mortgage amortized over 40 years is lower due to the longer amortization period and a lower average interest rate. The latter loan is more risky from a lender's point of view because the borrower's equity builds more slowly and the borrower will likely have to refinance after 30 years or have cash equal to 84 monthly payments. The monthly payment for the 2/28 ARM is documented in the third column. When the index interest rate remains constant, the payment increases by 14% in the month 25 at initial adjustment and by another 12% in month 31. When amortized over 40 years, as in the fourth column, the payment shock is more severe as the loan balance is much higher in every month compared to the 30-year amortization. In particular, the payment increases by 18% in month 25 and another 14% in month 31. However, when the 2/28 is combined with an interest-only option, the payment shock is even more severe since the principal balance does not decline at all over time when the borrower makes the minimum monthly payment. In this case, the payment increases by 19% in month 25, another 26% in month 31, and another 11% in month 61 when the interest-only option expires. The 3/27 ARMs exhibit similar patterns in monthly payments over time.

In order to better understand the severity of payment shock, Table 8 illustrates the impact of changes in the mortgage payment on the ratio of debt (service) to gross income. The table is constructed under the assumption that the borrower has no other debt than mortgage debt, and imposes an initial debt-to-income ratio of 40 percent, similar to that found in the mortgage pool. The third column documents that the debt-to-income ratio increases in month 31 to 50.45% for the simple 2/28 ARM, to 52.86% for the 2/28 ARM amortized over 40 years, and to 58.14% for the 2/28 ARM with an interest-only option. Without significant income growth over the first two years of the loan, it seems reasonable to expect that borrowers will struggle to make these higher payments. It begs the question why such a loan was made in the first place.

The likely answer is that lenders expected that the borrower would be able to refinance before payment reset.

Industry trends

Table 9 documents the average terms of loans securitized in the Alt-A and subprime markets over the last eight years. Subprime loans are more likely than Alt-A loans to be ARMs, and are largely dominated by the 2/28 and 3/27 hybrid ARMs. Subprime loans are less likely to have an interest-only option or permit negative amortization (i.e. option ARM), but are more likely to have a 40-year amortization instead of a 30-year amortization. The table also documents that hybrid ARMs have become more important over time for both Alt-A and subprime borrowers, as have interest only options and the 40-year amortization term. In the end, the mortgage pool referenced in our motivating example does not appear to be very different from the average loan securitized by the industry in 2006.

The immediate concern from the industry data is obviously the widespread dependency of subprime borrowers on what amounts to short-term funding, leaving them vulnerable to adverse shifts in the supply of subprime credit. Figure 3 documents the timing ARM resets over the next six years, as of January 2007. Given the dominance of the 2/28 ARM, it should not be surprising that the majority of loans that will be resetting over the next two years are subprime loans. The main source of uncertainty about the future performance of these loans is driven by uncertainty over the ability of these borrowers to refinance. This uncertainty has been highlighted by rapidly changing attitudes of investors towards subprime loans (see the box below on the ABX for the details). Regulators have released guidance on subprime loans that forces a lender to qualify a borrower on a fully-indexed and -amortizing interest rate and discourages the use of state-income loans. Moreover, recent changes in structuring criteria by the rating agencies have prompted several subprime lenders to stop originating hybrid ARMs. Finally, activity in the housing market has slowed down considerably, as the median price of existing homes has declined for the first time in decades while historical levels of inventory and vacant homes.

Table 6: Loan Type in the GSAMP 2006-NC2 Mortgage Loan Pool

Loan Type	Gross Rate	Margin	Initial Cap	Periodic Cap	Lifetime Cap	Floor	IO Period	Notional ($m)	% Total
FIXED	8.18	X	X	X	X	X	X	$ 79.12	8.98%
FIXED 40-year Balloon	7.58	X	X	X	X	X	X	$ 24.80	2.81%
2/28 ARM	8.64	6.22	1.49	1.49	15.62	8.62	X	$ 221.09	25.08%
2/28 ARM 40-year Balloon	8.31	6.24	1.5	1.5	15.31	8.31	X	$ 452.15	51.29%
2/28 ARM IO	7.75	6.13	1.5	1.5	14.75	7.75	60	$ 101.18	11.48%
3/27 ARM	7.48	6.06	1.5	1.5	14.48	7.48	X	$ 1.71	0.19%
3/27 ARM 40-year Balloon	7.61	6.11	1.5	1.5	14.61	7.61	X	$ 1.46	0.17%
Total	8.29	X	X	X	X	X	X	$ 881.50	100.00%

Note: LIBOR is 5.31% at the time of issue. Notional amount is reported in millions of dollars.
Source: SEC filings, Author's calculations

Table 7: Monthly Payment Across Mortgage Loan Type

Month	Monthly Payment Across Mortgage Loan Type						
	30-year fixed	30-year fixed	2/28 ARM	2/28 ARM	2/28 ARM IO	3/27 ARM	3/27 ARM
1	$ 1,633.87	$ 1,546.04	$ 1,701.37	$ 1,566.17	$ 1,404.01	$ 1,533.12	$ 1,437.35
24	1.00	1.00	1.00	1.00	1.00	1.00	1.00
25	1.00	1.00	1.14	1.18	1.19	1.00	1.00
30	1.00	1.00	1.14	1.18	1.19	1.00	1.00
31	1.00	1.00	1.26	1.32	1.45	1.00	1.00
36	1.00	1.00	1.26	1.32	1.45	1.00	1.00
37	1.00	1.00	1.26	1.32	1.45	1.13	1.18
42	1.00	1.00	1.26	1.32	1.45	1.13	1.18
43	1.00	1.00	1.26	1.32	1.45	1.27	1.34
48	1.00	1.00	1.26	1.32	1.45	1.27	1.34
49	1.00	1.00	1.26	1.32	1.45	1.27	1.43
60	1.00	1.00	1.26	1.32	1.45	1.27	1.43
61	1.00	1.00	1.26	1.32	1.56	1.27	1.43
359	1.00	1.00	1.26	1.32	1.56	1.27	1.43
360	1.00	83.81	1.26	100.72	1.56	1.27	105.60
Amortization	30 years	40 years	30 years	40 years	30 years	30 years	40 years

Note: The first line documents the average initial monthly payment for each loan type. The subsequent rows document the ratio of the future to the initial monthly payment under an assumption that LIBOR remains at 5.31% through the life of the loan.
Source: SEC filing, Author's Calculations

Table 8: Ratio of Debt to Income Across Mortgage Loan Type

Month	Ratio of Debt to Income Across Mortgage Loan Type						
	30-year fixed	30-year fixed	2/28 ARM	2/28 ARM	2/28 ARM IO	3/27 ARM	3/27 ARM
1	40.00%	40.00%	40.00%	40.00%	40.00%	40.00%	40.00%
24	40.00%	40.00%	40.00%	40.00%	40.00%	40.00%	40.00%
25	40.00%	40.00%	45.46%	47.28%	47.44%	40.00%	40.00%
30	40.00%	40.00%	45.46%	47.28%	47.44%	40.00%	40.00%
31	40.00%	40.00%	50.35%	52.86%	58.14%	40.00%	40.00%
36	40.00%	40.00%	50.35%	52.86%	58.14%	40.00%	40.00%
37	40.00%	40.00%	50.45%	52.86%	58.14%	45.36%	47.04%
42	40.00%	40.00%	50.45%	52.86%	58.14%	45.36%	47.04%
43	40.00%	40.00%	50.45%	52.86%	58.14%	50.83%	53.53%
48	40.00%	40.00%	50.45%	52.86%	58.14%	50.83%	53.53%
49	40.00%	40.00%	50.45%	52.86%	58.14%	50.83%	57.08%
60	40.00%	40.00%	50.45%	52.86%	58.14%	50.83%	57.08%
61	40.00%	40.00%	50.45%	52.86%	62.29%	50.83%	57.08%
359	40.00%	40.00%	50.45%	52.86%	62.29%	50.83%	57.08%
360	40.00%	3352.60%	50.45%	4028.64%	62.29%	50.83%	4223.92%
Amortization	30 years	40 years	30 years	40 years	30 years	30 years	40 years

Note: The table documents the path of the debt-to-income ratio over the life of each loan type under an assumption that LIBOR remains at 5.31% through the life of the loan. The calculation assumes that all debt is mortgage debt.
Source: SEC filing, Author's Calculations

Table 9: Terms of Mortgage Loans in MBS Pools

Year	ARM	2/28 ARM	3/27 ARM	5/25 ARM	IO	Option ARM	40-year
A. Alt-A							
1999	6.3	2.6	0.9	1.9	0.8	0.0	0.0
2000	12.8	4.7	1.7	3.4	1.1	1.1	0.1
2001	20.0	4.9	2.3	8.8	3.9	0.0	0.0
2002	28.0	3.7	2.8	10.9	7.7	0.4	0.0
2003	34.0	4.8	5.3	16.7	19.6	1.7	0.1
2004	68.7	8.9	16.7	24.0	46.4	10.3	0.5
2005	69.7	4.0	6.3	15.6	38.6	34.2	2.7
2006	69.8	1.8	1.7	15.8	35.6	42.3	11.0
B. Subprime							
1999	51.0	31.0	16.2	0.6	0.1	0.0	0.0
2000	64.5	45.5	16.6	0.6	0.0	0.1	0.0
2001	66.0	52.1	12.4	0.8	0.0	0.0	0.0
2002	71.6	57.4	12.1	1.4	0.7	0.0	0.0
2003	67.2	54.5	10.6	1.5	3.6	0.0	0.0
2004	78.0	61.3	14.7	1.6	15.3	0.0	0.0
2005	83.5	66.7	13.3	1.5	27.7	0.0	5.0
2006	81.7	68.7	10.0	2.5	18.1	0.0	26.9

Source: LoanPerformance (2007)

Figure 3: ARM reset schedule

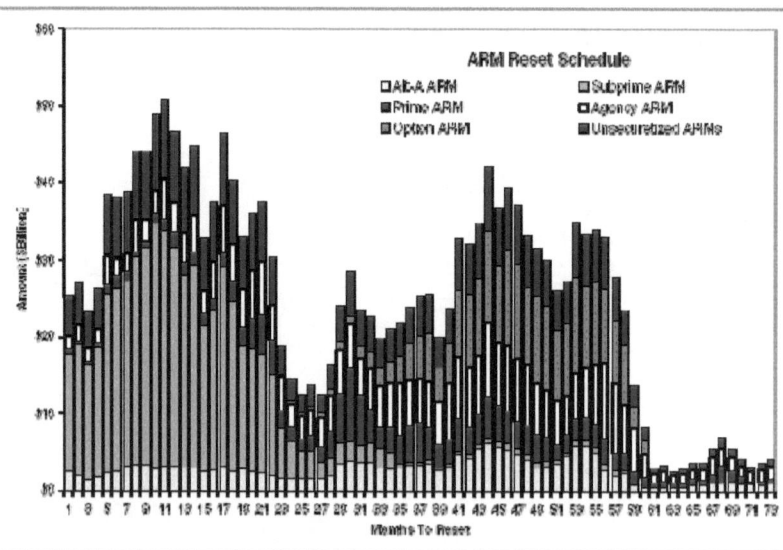

Note: Data as of January 2007.

Source: Credit Suisse Fixed Income U.S. Mortgage Strategy

The impact of payment reset on foreclosure

The most important issue facing the sub-prime credit market is obviously the impact of payment reset on the ability of borrowers to continue making monthly payments. Given that over three-fourths of the subprime-loans underwritten over 2004 to 2006 were hybrid ARMS, it is not difficult to understand the magnitude of the problem. But what is the likely outcome? The answer depends on a number of factors, including but not limited to: the amount of equity that these borrowers have in their homes at the time of reset (which itself is a function of CLTV at origination and the severity of the decline in home prices), the severity of payment reset (which depends not only on the loan but also on the six-month LIBOR interest rate), and of course conditions in the labor market.

A recent study by Cagan (2007) of mortgage payment reset tries to estimate what fraction of resetting loans will end up in foreclosure. The author presents evidence suggesting that in an environment of zero home price appreciation and full employment, 12 percent of subprime loans will default due to reset. We review the key elements of this analysis.[9]

Table 10 documents the amount of loans issued over 2004-2006 that were still outstanding as of March 2007, broken out by initial interest rate group and payment reset size group. The data includes all outstanding securitized mortgage loans with a future payment reset date. Each row corresponds to a different initial interest rate bucket: RED corresponding to loans with initial rates between 1 and 3.9 percent; YELLOW corresponding to an initial interest rate of 4.0 to 6.49 percent; and ORANGE with an initial interest rate of 6.5 to 12 percent. Subprime loans can be easily identified by the high original interest rate in the third row (ORANGE). Each column corresponds to a different payment reset size group under an assumption of no change in the 6-month LIBOR interest rate: A to payments which increase between 0 and 25 percent; B to payments which increase between 26 and 50 percent; C to payments which increase between 51 and 99 percent; and D to payments which increase by at least 100 percent. Note that almost all of subprime payment reset is in either the 0-25% or the 26-50% groups, with a little more than $300 billion in loans sitting in each group. There is a clear correlation in the table between the initial interest rate and the average size of the payment reset. The most severe payment resets appear to be the problem of Alt-A and Jumbo borrowers.

Table 10: Distribution of Loans by First Reset Size

	Reset size ($ billions)				
Initial interest rate	A (0-25%)	B (26-50%)	C (51-99%)	D (100%+)	Total
RED (1.0-3.9%)	$0	$0	$61	$460	$521
YELLOW (4.0-6.49%)	$545	$477	$102	$0	$1,124
ORANGE (6.5-12%)	$366	$316	$49	$0	$631
Total	$811	$793	$212	$460	$2,276

Source: Cagan (2007); data refer to all ARMs originated 2004-2006.

Cagan helpfully provides estimates of the distribution of updated equity across the initial interest rate group in Table 11. The author uses an automated appraisal system in order to estimate the value of each property, and then constructs an updated value of the equity for each

---

[9] The author is a PhD economist at First American, a credit union which owns LoanPerformance.

borrower. The table reports the cumulative distribution of equity for each initial interest rate bucket reported in the table above. Note that 22.4 percent of subprime borrowers (ORANGE) are estimated to have no equity in their homes, about half have no more than 10 percent, and two-thirds have less than 20 percent. Disturbingly, the table suggests that a national price decline of 10 percent could put half of all subprime borrowers underwater.

Table 11: Cumulative distribution of equity by initial interest rate

Equity	Initial Rate Group		
	Red	Yellow	Orange
<-20%	2.2%	1.5%	2.7%
<-15%	3.2	2.0	4.0
<-10%	4.9	2.9	6.2
<-5%	8.2	4.8	11.6
<0%	14.1	8.6	22.4
<5%	23.9	15.5	36.0
<10%	36.7	24.5	47.7
<15%	49.7	34.7	57.9
<20%	62.4	45.4	67.3
<25%	73.3	56.8	76.8
<30%	81.3	67.5	84.6

Source: Cagan (2007); data refer to all ARMs originated 2004-2006.

In order to transform this raw data into estimates of foreclosure due to reset, the author makes assumptions in Table 12 about the amount of equity or the size of payment reset and the probability of foreclosures.[10] A borrower will only default given difficulty with payment reset and difficulty in refinancing. For example, 70% of borrowers with equity between -5% and 5% are assumed to face difficulty refinancing, while only 30% of borrowers with equity between 15% and 25% have difficulty. At the same time, the author assumes that only 10 percent of borrowers with payment reset 0-25% will face difficulty with the higher payment, while 70 percent with a payment reset of 51-99% will be unable to make the higher payment.

Table 12: Assumed probability of default by reset size and equity risk group

		Reset Size Group			
		A	B	C	D
		25% or less	26-50%	51-99%	100% or more
Equity	Pr(difficulty)	10%	40%	70%	100%
>25%	10%	1%	4%	7%	10%
15-25%	30%	3	12	21	30
5-15%	50%	5	20	35	50
-5-5%	70%	7	28	49	70
<-5%	90%	9	36	63	90

Source: Cagan (2007).

Estimates of foreclosure due to reset in an environment of constant home prices are documented in Table 13. The author estimates that foreclosures due to reset will be 3.5% (= 106.2/3033.1) for the 0-25% reset group and 13.5% (= 446.4/3282.8) for the 26-50% group.

---

[10] The author offers no rationale for these figures, but the analysis here should be transparent enough that one could use different inputs to construct their own alternative scenarios.

Given the greater equity risk of subprime mortgages documented in Table 11, a back-of-the-envelope calculation suggests that these numbers would be 4.5% and 18.6% for subprime mortgages.

Table 13: Summary of foreclosure estimates under 0% home price appreciation

Reset Size	Reset Risk	Equity Risk	Pr(loss)	Loans (t)	Foreclosures (t)
A (25% or less)	10%	35%	3.5%	3033.1	106.2
B (26-50%)	40%	34%	13.6%	3282.8	446.4
C (51-99%)	70%	31%	21.7%	839.2	182.1
D (100% or more)	100%	36%	36.0%	1,216.7	438.0
			Total	8,371.9	1,172.7
			Percent foreclosures		14.0%

Source: Cagan (2007).

The author also investigates a scenario where home prices fall by 10 percent in Table 14, and estimates foreclosures due to reset for the two payment reset size groups to be 5.5% and 21.6%, respectively. Note that the revised July 2007 economic forecast for Moody's called for this exact scenario by the end of 2008.

Table 14: Summary of foreclosure estimates under 10% national home price decline

Reset Size	Reset Risk	Equity Risk	Pr(loss)	Loans (t)	Foreclosures (t)
A (25% or less)	10%	55%	5.5%	3033.1	166.8
B (26-50%)	40%	54%	21.6%	3282.8	709.1
C (51-99%)	70%	51%	35.7%	839.2	299.6
D (100% or more)	100%	56%	56.0%	1,216.7	681.3
			Total	8,371.9	1856.8
			Percent foreclosures		22.2%

Source: Cagan (2007).

Market conditions have deteriorated dramatically since this study was published, as the origination of both sub-prime and Alt-A mortgage loans has all but disappeared, making the author's assumptions about equity risk even in the stress scenario for home prices look optimistic. Moreover, the author's original assumption that reset risk is constant across the credit spectrum is likely to be optimistic. In particular, sub-prime borrowers are less likely to be able to handle payment reset, resulting with estimates of foreclosures that are quite modest relative to those in the research reports of investment banks.

3.3. How have subprime loans performed?

Motivating example

Table 15 documents how the GSAMP 2006-NC2 deal has performed through August 2007. The first three columns report mortgage loans still in the pool that are 30-days, 60-days, and 90-days past due. The fourth column reports loans that are in foreclosure. The fifth column reports loans where the bank has title to the property. The sixth column reports actual cumulative losses. The last column documents the fraction of original loans that remain in the pool.

Table 15: Performance of GSAMP 2006-NC2

Date	30 day	60 day	90 day	Foreclosure	Bankruptcy	REO	Cum Loss	CPR	Principal
Aug-07	6.32%	3.39%	1.70%	7.60%	0.90%	3.66%	0.25%	20.35%	72.48%
Jul-07	5.77%	3.47%	1.31%	7.31%	1.03%	3.15%	0.20%	20.77%	73.90%
Jun-07	5.61%	3.09%	1.43%	6.92%	0.70%	2.63%	0.10%	25.26%	75.38%
May-07	4.91%	3.34%	1.38%	6.48%	0.78%	1.83%	0.08%	19.18%	77.26%
Apr-07	4.68%	3.38%	1.16%	6.77%	0.50%	0.72%	0.04%	15.71%	78.68%
Mar-07	4.74%	2.77%	1.12%	6.76%	0.38%	0.21%	0.02%	19.03%	79.84%
Feb-07	4.79%	2.59%	0.96%	6.00%	0.37%	0.03%	0.00%	23.08%	81.29%
Jan-07	4.58%	2.85%	0.88%	5.04%	0.36%	0.00%	0.00%	28.54%	83.12%

Source: ABSNet

What do these numbers imply for the expected performance of the mortgage pool. UBS (June 2007) outlines an approach to use actual deal performance in order to estimate lifetime losses. Using historical data on loans in an environment of low home price appreciation (less than 5 percent), the author documents that approximately 70 percent of loans in the 60-day, 90-day, and bankruptcy categories eventually default, defined as the event of foreclosure. Interestingly, only about 60-70 percent of loans in bankruptcy are actually delinquent. Moreover, these transitions into foreclosure take about 4 months.

The amount of default "in the pipeline" for remaining loans in the next four months is constructed as follows:

Pipeline default = $0.7 \times$ (60-day + 90-day + bankruptcy)
   + (foreclosure + real-estate owned)

For GSAMP 2006-NC2, the pipeline default from the August report is 15.45%, suggesting that this fraction of loans remaining in the pool are likely to default in the next four months.

Total default is constructed by combining this measure with the fraction of loans remaining in the pool, actual cumulative losses to date, and an assumption about the severity of loss. In the UBS study, the author assumes a loss given default of 37%.

Total default = pipeline default $\times$ (fraction of loans remaining) + (Cum loss)/(loss severity)

For the GSAMP 2006-NC2, this number is 11.88%, which suggests that this fraction of the original pool will have defaulted in four months.

Finally, the paper uses historical data in order to estimate the fraction of total defaults over the life of deal. In particular, a mapping is constructed between weighted-average loan age and the fraction of lifetime default that a deal typically realizes. For example, the typical deal realizes 33% of its defaults by month 13, 59% by month 23, 75% by month 35, and 100% by month 60.

Projected cumulative default = Total default/Default timing factor

The New Century pool was originated in May 2006, implying that the average loan is about 16 months old at the end of August 2007. The default timing factor for 20 months, which must be used since defaults were predicted through four months in the future, is 51.2%, suggesting that projected cumulative default on this mortgage pool is 23.19%. Using a loss severity of 37% results in expected lifetime loss on this mortgage pool of 8.58%.

There are several potential weaknesses of this approach, the foremost being the fact that it is backward-looking and essentially ignores the elephant in the room, payment reset. In particular, in the fact of payment reset, losses are likely to be more back-loaded than the historical curve used above, implying the fraction of lifetime losses which have been observed to date is likely to be too small, resulting in lifetime loss estimates which are too low. In order to address this problem, UBS (23 October 2007) has developed a shut-down model to take into account the inability of borrowers to refinance their way out of payment resets. In that article, the authors estimate the lower prepayment speeds associate with refinancing stress will increase losses by an average of 50 percent. Moreover, the authors also speculate that loss severities will be higher than the 37 percent used above, and incorporate an assumption of 45 percent. Together, these assumptions imply that a more conservative view on losses would be to scale those from the loss projection model above by a factor of two, implying a lifetime loss rate of 17.16% on the example pool.

Industry

UBS (June 2007) applies this methodology to home equity ABS deals that constitute three vintages of the ABX: 06-1, 06-2, and 07-1. In order to understand the jargon, note that deals in 06-1 refer mortgages that were largely originated in the second half of 2005, while deals in 06-2 refer to mortgages that were largely underwritten in the first half of 2006.

Figure 4 illustrates estimates of the probability distribution of estimated losses as of the June remittance reports across the 20 different deals for each of the three vintages of loans. The mean loss rate of the 06-1 vintage is 5.6%, while the mean of the 06-2 and 07-1 vintages are 9.2% and 11.7%, respectively. From the figure, it is clear that not only the mean but also the variance of the distribution of losses at the deal level has increased considerably over the last year. Moreover, expected lifetime losses from the New Century securitization studied in the example are a little lower than the average deal in the ABX from 06-2.

Figure 4: Subprime Projected Losses by Vintage

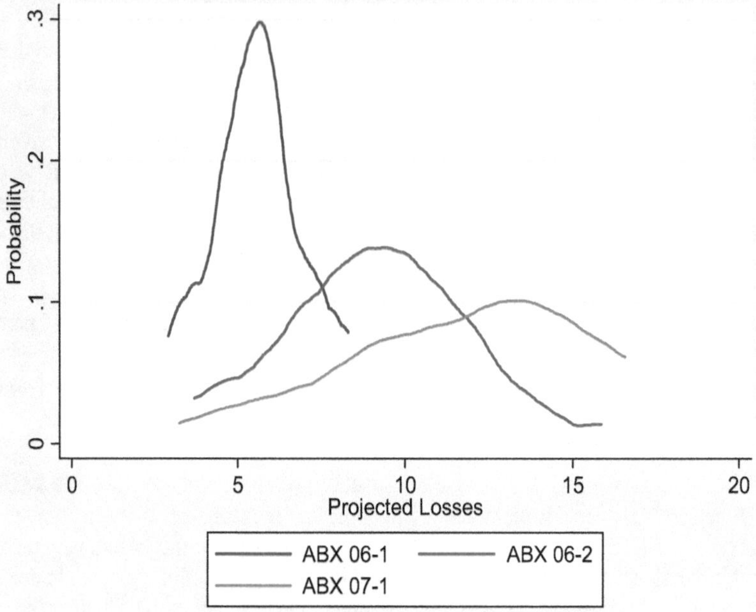

```
                    ABX 06-1 ———    ABX 06-2
                    ABX 07-1
```

3.4. How are subprime loans valued?

In January 2006, Markit launched the ABX, which is a series of indices that track the price of credit default insurance on a standardized basket of home equity ABS obligations.[11] The ABX actually has five indices, differentiated by credit rating: AAA, AA, A, BBB, and BBB-. Each of these indices is an equally-weighted average of the price of credit insurance at a maturity of 30-years across similarly-rated tranches from 20 different home equity ABS deals. For example, the BBB index tracks the average price of credit default insurance on the BBB-rated tranche.

Every six months, a new set of 20 home equity deals is chosen from the largest dealer shelves in the previous half year. In order to ensure proper diversification in the portfolio, the same originator is limited to no more than four deals and the same master servicer is limited to no more than six deals. Each reference obligation must be rated by both Moody's and S&P and have a weighted-average remaining life of 4-6 years.

In a typical transaction, a protection buyer pays the protection seller a fixed coupon at a monthly rate on an amount determined by the buyer. For example, Table 16 documents that the price of protection on the AAA tranche of the most recent vintage (07-2) is a coupon rate of 76

---

[11] In the jargon, first-lien sub-prime mortgage loans as well as second- lien home equity loans and home equity lines of credit (HELCOs) are all part of what is called the Home Equity ABS sector. First- lien Alt-A and Jumbo loans are part of what is called the Residential Mortgage-backed Securities (RMBS) sector.

basis points per year. Note the significant increase in coupons on all tranches between 07-1 and 07-2, which reflects a significant change in investor sentiment from January to Jul 2007.

When a credit event occurs, the protection seller makes a payment to the protection buyer in an amount equal to the loss. Credit events include the shortfall of interest or principal (i.e. the servicer fails to forward a payment when it is due) as well as the write-down of the tranche due to losses on underlying mortgage loans. In the event that these losses are later reimbursed, the protection buyer must reimburse the protection seller.

For example, if one tranche of a securitization referenced in the index is written down by an amount of 1%, and the current balance of the tranche is 70% of its original balance, an institution which has sold $10 million in protection must make a payment of $583,333 [= $10m × 70% × (1/20)] to the protection buyer. Moreover, the future protection fee will be based on a principal balance that is 0.20% [= 1% × (1/20)] lower than before the write-down of the tranche.

Changes in investor views about the risk of the mortgage loans over time will affect the price at which investors are willing to buy or sell credit protection. However, the terms of the insurance contract (i.e. coupon, maturity, pool of deals) are fixed. The ABX tracks the amount that one party has to pay the other at the onset of the contract in order for both parties to accept the terms. For example, when investors think the underlying loans have become more risky since the index was created, a protection buyer will have to pay an up-front fee to the protection seller in order to only pay a coupon of 76 basis points per year. On 24 July, the ABX.AAA.07 was at 98.04, suggesting that a protection buyer would have to pay the seller a fee of 1.96% up-front. Using an estimate of 5.19 from UBS of this tranche's estimated duration, it is possible to write the implied spread on the tranche as 114 basis points per year [= 100 × (100 - 98.04)/5.19 + 76].

Figure 5 documents the behavior of the BBB-rated 06-2 vintage of the ABX over the first six and a half months of 2007. Note from Table 16 that the initial coupon on this tranche was 133 basis points. However, the first two months of the year marked a significant adverse change in investor sentiment against the home equity sector. In particular, the BBB-rated index fell from 95 to below 75 by the end of February. Using an estimated duration of 3.3, the implied spread increased from just under 300 basis points to almost 900 basis points. Through the end of May, this index fluctuated between 80 and 85, consistent with an implied spread of about 650 basis points. However, the market responded adversely to a further deterioration in performance following the May remittance report, and at the time of this writing, the index has dropped to about 54, consistent with an implied spread of approximately 1800 basis points.

While it is not clear what exactly triggered the sell-off in the first two months of January, there were some notable events that occurred over this period. There were early concerns about the vintage in the form of early payment defaults resulting in originators being forced to repurchase loans from securitizations. These repurchase requests put pressure on the liquidity of originators. Moreover, warehouse lenders began to ask for more collateral, putting further liquidity pressure on originators.

Table 16: Overview of the ABX Index

Vintage	Credit Rating	Coupon Rate	Index Price	Estimated Duration	Implied Spread
07-2	AAA	76	98.04	5.19	114
07-2	AA	192	95.36	3.85	313
07-2	A	369	78.05	3.47	1002
07-2	BBB	500	54.43	3.31	1877
07-2	BBB-	500	47.31	3.30	2097
07-1	AAA	9	95.05	5.07	107
07-1	AA	15	88.36	3.7	330
07-1	A	64	65.5	3.44	1067
07-1	BBB	224	44.55	3.02	2060
07-1	BBB-	389	41.79	2.75	2506
06-2	AAA	11	96.45	4.68	87
06-2	AA	17	92.79	3.21	242
06-2	A	44	74.45	3.05	882
06-2	BBB	133	53.57	2.77	1809
06-2	BBB-	242	46.75	2.53	2347
06-1	AAA	18	99.04	4.27	40
06-1	AA	32	97.82	2.89	107
06-1	A	54	85.04	2.74	600
06-1	BBB	154	74.79	2.57	1135
06-1	BBB-	267	66.93	2.42	1634

Source: Coupon and Price: Markit (24 July 2007); duration: UBS; Implied spread is author's calculation as follows: implied spread = 100*[100-price]/duration + coupon rate.

Figure 5: ABX.BBB 06-2

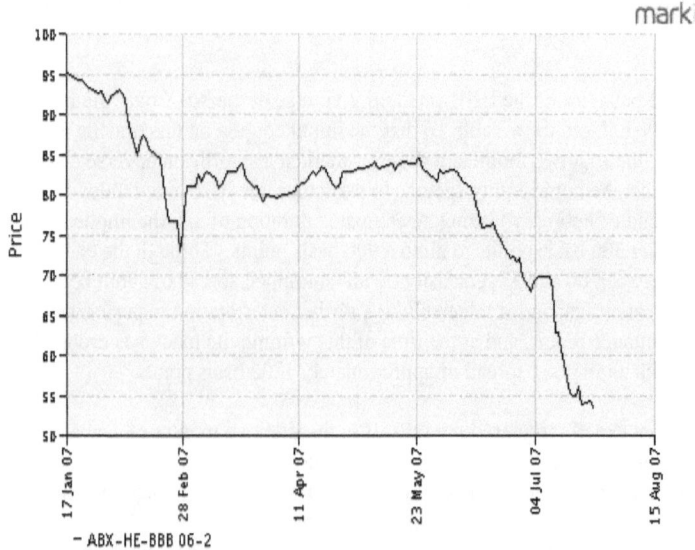

Source: Markit

4. Overview of subprime MBS

The typical subprime trust has the following structural features designed to protect investors from losses on the underlying mortgage loans:

- Subordination
- Excess spread
- Shifting interest
- Performance triggers
- Interest rate swap

We discuss each of these forms of credit enhancement in turn.

4.1. Subordination

The distribution of losses on the mortgage pool is typically tranched into different classes. In particular, losses on the mortgage loan pool are applied first to the most junior class of investors until the principal balance of that class is completely exhausted. At that point, losses are allocated to the most junior class remaining, and so on.

The most junior class of a securitization is referred to as the equity tranche. In the case of subprime mortgage loans, the equity tranche is typically created through over-collateralization (o/c), which means that the principal balance of the mortgage loans exceeds the principal balance of all the debt issued by the trust. This is an important form of credit enhancement that is funded by the arranger in part through the premium it receives on offered securities. O/C is used to reduce the exposure of debt investors to loss on the pool mortgage loans.

A small part of the capital structure of the trust is made up of the mezzanine class of debt securities, which are next in line to absorb losses once the o/c is exhausted. This class of securities typically has several tranches with credit ratings that vary between AA and B. With greater risk comes greater return, as these securities pay the highest interest rates to investors. The lion's share of the capital structure is always funded by the senior class of debt securities, which are last in line to absorb losses. Senior securities are protected not only by o/c, but also by the width of the mezzanine class. In general, the sum of o/c and the width of all tranches junior is referred to as subordination. Senior securities generally have the highest rating, and since they are last in line (to absorb losses), pay the lowest interest rates to investors.

Table 17: Capital structure of GSAMP Trust 2006-NC2

Class	Tranche description			Credit Ratings		Coupon Rate	
	Notional	Width	Subordination	S&P	Moody's	(1)	(2)
A-1	$239,618,000	27.18%	72.82%	AAA	Aaa	0.15%	0.30%
A-2A	$214,090,000	24.29%	48.53%	AAA	Aaa	0.07%	0.14%
A-2B	$102,864,000	11.67%	36.86%	AAA	Aaa	0.09%	0.18%
A-2C	$99,900,000	11.33%	25.53%	AAA	Aaa	0.15%	0.30%
A-2D	$42,998,000	4.88%	20.65%	AAA	Aaa	0.24%	0.48%
M-1	$35,700,000	4.05%	16.60%	AA+	Aa1	0.30%	0.45%
M-2	$28,649,000	3.25%	13.35%	AA	Aa2	0.31%	0.47%
M-3	$16,748,000	1.90%	11.45%	AA-	Aa3	0.32%	0.48%
M-4	$14,986,000	1.70%	9.75%	A+	A1	0.35%	0.53%
M-5	$14,545,000	1.65%	8.10%	A	A2	0.37%	0.56%
M-6	$13,663,000	1.55%	6.55%	A-	A3	0.46%	0.69%
M-7	$12,341,000	1.40%	5.15%	BBB+	Baa1	0.90%	1.35%
M-8	$11,019,000	1.25%	3.90%	BBB	Baa2	1.00%	1.50%
M-9	$7,052,000	0.80%	3.10%	BBB-	Baa3	2.05%	3.08%
B-1	$6,170,000	0.70%	2.40%	BB+	Ba1	2.50%	3.75%
B-2	$8,815,000	1.00%	1.40%	BB	Ba2	2.50%	3.75%
X	$12,340,995	1.40%	0.00%	NR	NR	N/A	N/A

Source: Prospectus filed with the SEC of GSAMP 2006-NC2

Figure 6: Typical Capital Structure of Subprime and Alt-A MBS

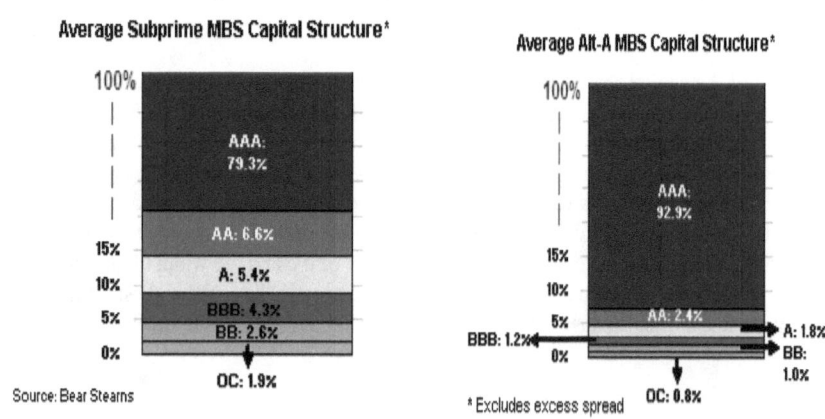

The capital structure of GSAMP 2006-NC1 is illustrated in Table 17. First, note that the o/c is the class X, which represents 1.4% of the principal balance of the mortgages. There are two B classes of securities not offered in the prospectus. The mezzanine class benefits from a total of 3.10% of subordination created by the o/c and the class B securities. However, note that the mezzanine class is split up into 9 different classes, M-1 to M-10, which class M-2 being junior to class M-1, etc. For example, the M-8 class tranche, which has an investment grade-rating of BBB, has subordination of 3.9% and pays a coupon of 100 basis points. Investors receive 1/12 of this amount on the distribution date, which is the 25th of each month. The senior class benefits from 20.65% of total subordination, including the width of the mezzanine class (19.25%).

Note that the New Century structure is broken into two groups of Class A securities, corresponding to two sub-pools of the mortgage loans. In Group I loans, every mortgage has original principal balance lower than the GSE-conforming loan limits. This feature permits the GSEs to purchase these Class A-1 securities. However, in the Group II loans, there is a mixture of mortgage loans with original principal balance above and below the GSE-conforming loan limit.

The table does not mention either the class P or class C certificates, which have no face value and are not entitled to distributions of principal or interest. The class P securities are the sole beneficiary of all future prepayment penalties. Since the arranger will be paid for these rights, it reduces the premium needed on other offered securities for the deal to work. The class C securities contain a clean-up option which permits the trust to call the offered securities should the principal balance of the mortgage pool fall to a sufficiently low level.[12] In our example deal, the offered debt securities are rated by both S&P and Moody's. Note that Table 17 documents that there is no disagreement between the agencies in their opinion of the appropriate credit rating for each tranche.

4.2. Excess spread

Subordination is not the only protection that senior and mezzanine tranche investors have against loss. As an example, the weighted average coupon from the mortgage loan will typically be larger than fees to the servicers, net payments to the swap counterparty, and the weighted average coupon on debt securities issued by the trust. This difference is referred to as excess spread, which is used to absorb credit losses on the mortgage loans, with the remainder distributed each month to the owners of the Class X securities. Note that this is the first line of defense for investors for credit losses, as the principal of no tranche is reduced by any amount until credit losses reduce excess spread to a negative number. The amount of credit enhancement provided by excess spread depends on both the severity as well as the timing of losses.

In the New Century deal, the weighted average coupon on the tranches at origination is LIBOR plus 23 basis points. With LIBOR at 5.32% at the time of issue, this implies an interest cost of 5.55%. In addition to this cost, the trust pays 51 basis points in servicing fees and initially pays 13 basis points to the swap counterparty (see below). As the weighted average interest rate on collateral at the time of issue is 8.30%, the initial excess spread on this mortgage pool is 2.11%.

More generally, the amount of excess spread varies by deal, but averaged about 2.5 percent during 2006. Dealers estimate that loss rates must reach 9 percent before the average BBB minus bond sustains its first dollar of principal loss, about twice its initial subordination of 4.5 percent in Figure 6 above.

---

[12] The figure also omits discussion of certain "residual certificates" that are not entitled to distributions of interest but appear to be related to residual ownership interests in assets of the trust.

4.3. Shifting interest

Senior investors are also protected by the practice of shifting interest, which requires that all principal payments to be applied to senior notes over a specified period of time (usually the first 36 months) before being paid to mezzanine bondholders. During this time, known as the "lockout period," mezzanine bondholders receive only the coupon on their notes. As the principal of senior notes is paid down, the ratio of the senior class to the balance of the entire deal (senior interest) decreases during the first couple years, hence the term "shifting interest". The amount of subordination (alternatively, credit enhancement) for the senior class increases over time because the amount of senior bonds outstanding is smaller relative to the amount outstanding for mezzanine bonds.

4.4. Performance triggers

After the lockout period, subject to passing performance tests,[13] the o/c is released and principal is applied to mezzanine notes from the bottom of the capital structure up until target levels of subordination are reached (usually twice the initial subordination, as a percent of current balance). In addition to protecting senior note holders, the purpose of the shifting interest mechanism is to adjust subordination across the capital structure after sufficient seasoning. Also, the release of o/c and pay-down of mezzanine notes reduces the average life of these bonds and the interest costs of the securitization.

In our example securitization, o/c is specified to be 1.4% of the principal balance of the mortgage loans as of the cutoff-date, at least until the step-down date. The step-down date is the earlier of the date on which the principal balance of the senior class has been reduced to zero and the later to occur of 36 months or subordination of the senior class being greater than or equal to 41.3% of the aggregate principal balance of remaining mortgage loans. The trigger event is defined as a distribution date when one of the following two conditions is met:

- The rolling three-month average of 60-days or more delinquent (including those in foreclosure, REO properties, or mortgage loans in bankruptcy) divided by the remaining principal balance of the mortgage loans is larger than 38.70% of the subordination of the senior class from the previous month; or,
- The amount of cumulative realized losses incurred over the life of the deal as a fraction of the original principal balance of the mortgage loans exceeds the thresholds in Figure 7.

If the trigger event does not occur, the deal is 36 months old, and the subordination of the senior class is larger than 41.3%, then the deal will step-down. In this case, o/c is specified to be 2.8 percent of the principal balance of the mortgage loans in the previous month, subject to a floor equal to 0.5% of the principal balance of the mortgage loans as of the cut-off date. At this time, any excess o/c is released to holders of the Class X tranche. Note that the trigger event only affects whether or not o/c is released.

---

[13] There are two types of performance tests in subprime deals, one testing the deal's cumulative losses against a loss schedule, and another test for 60+ day delinquencies.

4.5. Interest rate swap

While most of the loans are ARMs, as discussed above, the interest rates will not adjust for two to three years following origination. It follows that the trust is exposed to the risk that interest rates increase, so that the cost of funding increases faster than interest payments received on the mortgages. In order to mitigate this risk, the trust engages in an interest rate swap with a third-party named the swap counterparty. In particular, the third-party has agreed to accept a sequence of fixed payments in return for promising to send a sequence of adjustable-rate payments.

In our example, Goldman Sachs is the Swap counterparty, which has agreed to pay 1-month LIBOR and accept a fixed interest rate of 5.45% on a notional amount described in Figure 8 over a term of 60 months. Note that the notional amount hedged decreases over time, as the trust expects pre-payments of principal on the pool of mortgage loans to reduce the amount of debt securities outstanding.

Figure 7: Cumulative Loss Thresholds for GSAMP Trust 2006-NC2 Trigger Event

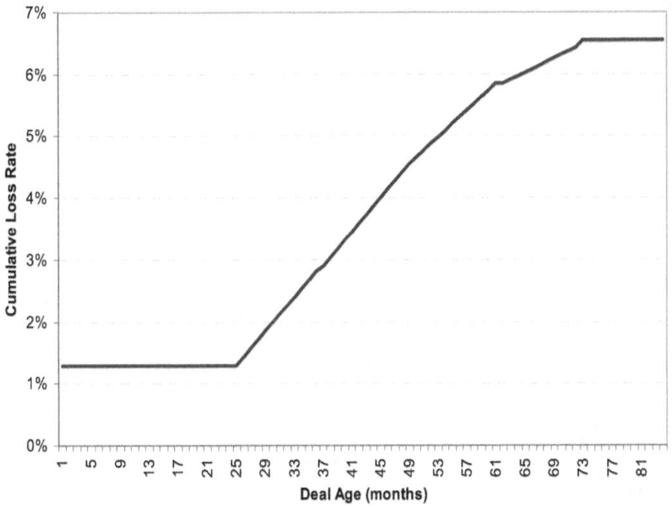

Source: SEC Prospectus for GSAMP Trust 2006-NC2

Figure 8: Schedule of Interest Swap Notional for GSAMP Trust 2006-NC2

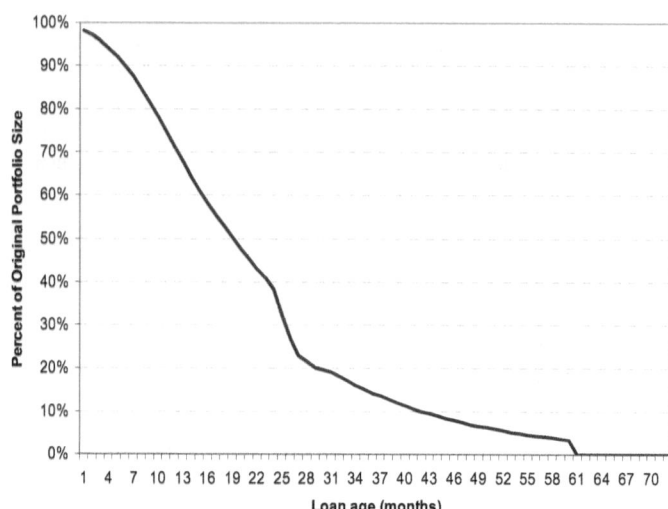

Source: SEC Prospectus for GSAMP Trust 2006-NC2

4.6 Remittance reports

The trustee makes monthly reports to investors known as remittance reports. In this section, we use data from these reports in order to document the performance of the New Century deal through August 2007.

Table 18 documents cash receipts of the trust. Scheduled principal and interest are collected from a borrower's monthly payment. Unscheduled principal is collected from borrowers who pay more than their required monthly payment, as well as borrowers who either pre-pay or default on their loans. The first three columns of the table report the remittance of scheduled and unscheduled principal as well as interest and pre-payment penalties. The fourth column reports advances of principal and interest made to the trust by the servicer to cover the non-payment of these items by certain borrowers. The fifth column documents the repurchase of loans by New Century which have been determined to violate the originator's representations and warranties. Note that only one loan has been repurchased with a principal balance of $184,956 as of this writing. Finally, realized losses are reported in the sixth column.

Table 18: GSAMP Trust 2006-NC2 cash receipts

Date	Remittances of principal		Remittances of interest and prepayment penalties	Servicer Advances	Loan Repurchases	Realized losses	Deposits
	Scheduled	Unscheduled					
Jul-06	$329,304	$9,067,656	$5,860,567	$233,039	$0	$0	$15,561,090
Aug-06	$328,927	$11,818,842	$5,772,726	$483,778	$0	$0	$18,492,964
Sep-06	$328,005	$18,872,868	$5,099,068	$1,317,531	$0	$0	$25,783,064
Oct-06	$324,632	$21,123,948	$5,874,901	$1,230,848	$0	$0	$28,870,206
Nov-06	$320,165	$21,913,838	$5,669,909	$1,191,300	$0	$0	$29,496,641
Dec-06	$315,176	$42,949,370	$5,496,644	$1,174,086	$0	$0	$50,229,238
Jan-06	$303,981	$20,805,981	$4,992,533	$1,342,346	$0	$0	$27,717,274
Feb-06	$298,715	$15,842,586	$4,874,742	$1,293,706	$184,956	-$1,162	$22,738,857
Mar-06	$294,018	$12,488,956	$4,845,576	$1,346,264	$0	-$179,720	$18,945,495
Apr-06	$292,054	$9,947,596	$4,781,758	$1,369,108	$0	-$166,703	$16,351,873
May-06	$290,315	$12,190,508	$4,605,848	$1,493,314	$0	-$323,425	$18,459,415
Jun-06	$285,113	$16,320,384	$4,554,347	$1,577,756	$0	-$233,174	$22,742,178
Jul-06	$279,953	$12,764,719	$4,386,611	$1,712,117	$0	-$835,539	$18,504,802
Aug-06	$275,885	$12,226,786	$4,425,290	$1,720,552	$0	-$459,357	$18,380,129

Source: remittance reports through ABSNet

Table 19 documents the cash expenses of the trust. The net swap payments are reported in the first column. Recall that the trust pays Goldman Sachs a fixed interest rate of 5.45 percent and receives an amount equal to one-month LIBOR, each on the amount referenced by Table 18 above. The servicer fees are based on the outstanding principal balance of the mortgage loans at the end of the last month, with 50 basis points paid to the servicer (Owcen) and just under 1 basis point paid to the master servicer (Wells Fargo). All principal paid by the borrower is advanced to the holders of Class A certificates. Each tranche is paid the stated coupon from Table 18 above based on the amount outstanding at the end of the previous month. Prepayment penalties are paid to the owners of the Class P tranche. The residual is denoted excess spread, and is paid to the owners of the Class X tranche each month.

The face value of the Class X tranche is $12.3 million. To date, this tranche has been paid excess spread in the amount of $16.1 million. Note that the amount paid to this tranche has decreased over time as credit losses have reduced excess spread. Interestingly, even if the owners of this class are not paid another dollar of interest, they will have received an amount equal to 130.9% of par.[14]

Table 19: Trust cash outlays

Date	Net Swap payments	Servicing fees	Servicer advance reimbursements	LIBOR certificate		Prepayment penalties	Excess Spread
				Principal	Interest		
Jul-06	$62,518	$374,270	$0	$9,396,455	$3,503,784	$70,524	$2,153,539
Aug-06	$47,927	$370,280	$233,039	$12,147,768	$4,159,454	$88,691	$1,445,805
Sep-06	$91,323	$365,123	$483,778	$19,200,881	$4,058,029	$165,593	$1,418,337
Oct-06	$82,957	$356,970	$1,317,531	$21,448,581	$3,844,241	$315,875	$1,504,051
Nov-06	$96,794	$347,863	$1,230,848	$22,234,002	$4,114,629	$401,429	$1,071,070
Dec-06	$82,988	$338,423	$1,191,300	$43,264,545	$3,518,752	$293,963	$1,539,266
Jan-06	$64,178	$320,054	$1,174,086	$21,109,962	$3,463,517	$272,433	$1,313,044
Feb-06	$86,137	$311,091	$1,342,346	$16,141,301	$3,573,069	$245,315	$1,039,598
Mar-06	$72,641	$304,238	$1,293,706	$12,782,974	$3,058,328	$150,401	$1,283,208
Apr-06	$74,677	$298,810	$1,346,264	$10,239,650	$3,219,019	$128,060	$1,045,393
May-06	$71,316	$294,463	$1,369,108	$12,480,823	$3,172,768	$202,855	$868,082
Jun-06	$70,108	$289,163	$1,493,314	$16,605,497	$3,220,305	$237,753	$826,037
Jul-06	$64,543	$282,113	$1,577,756	$13,044,672	$3,041,335	$196,941	$297,443
Aug-06	$67,536	$276,574	$1,712,117	$12,502,671	$3,280,603	$190,972	$349,654

Source: remittance reports from ABSNet

---

[14] Note given the amount of cash being paid out to equity tranche investors in such a bad state of nature, it is likely that these investors have paid a premium over par for these securities, so this should not be interpreted as a return.

There are two trigger events which prevent the release of over-collateralization at the step-down date, as shown in Table 20. The trigger amount in the third column for the 3-month moving average of 60-day delinquencies is 38.7 percent of the previous month's senior enhancement percentage reported in the fourth column. Recall that the trigger amount for the cumulative losses is constant at 1.3 percent over the first two years of the deal. While losses to date remain lower than the loss trigger amount, the 3-month moving average of 60-day delinquencies has been larger than the threshold amount since the April 2007 remittance report.

Table 20: Key triggers

Date	LIBOR 1-month	Moving Average 60d Delinquency		Senior Enhancement		Cumulative Loss	
		Amount	Trigger	Amount	Specified	Amount	Trigger
Jul-06	5.35%	0.04%	7.99%	20.87%	41.30%	0.00%	1.30%
Aug-06	5.38%	0.02%	8.08%	21.17%	41.30%	0.00%	1.30%
Sep-06	5.32%	0.78%	8.19%	21.65%	41.30%	0.00%	1.30%
Oct-06	5.33%	2.32%	8.38%	22.22%	41.30%	0.00%	1.30%
Nov-06	5.32%	4.84%	8.60%	22.84%	41.30%	0.00%	1.30%
Dec-06	5.32%	6.42%	8.84%	24.18%	41.30%	0.00%	1.30%
Jan-06	5.35%	7.97%	9.35%	24.84%	41.30%	0.00%	1.30%
Feb-06	5.32%	9.12%	9.61%	25.40%	41.30%	0.00%	1.30%
Mar-06	5.32%	4.47%	9.83%	25.86%	41.30%	0.02%	1.30%
Apr-06	5.32%	12.62%	10.10%	26.25%	41.30%	0.04%	1.30%
May-06	5.32%	14.32%	10.16%	26.73%	41.30%	0.08%	1.30%
Jun-06	5.32%	16.07%	10.34%	27.40%	41.30%	0.10%	1.30%
Jul-06	5.32%	17.83%	10.60%	27.94%	41.30%	0.19%	1.30%
Aug-06	5.32%	19.66%	10.81%	28.49%	41.30%	0.24%	1.30%

Source: remittance reports from ABSnet

The remittance report also discloses loan modifications performed by the servicer each month. Note that through the August remittance report, there have been no modifications of any mortgage loan in the pool. This is not surprising as the first payment reset date for these 2/28 ARMs will not be until spring 2008.

Finally, the remittance report also discloses information that permits a calculation of loss severity. At the time of this writing, the trust has incurred a loss of $2.199 million on 44 mortgage loans with principal balance of $5.042 million, for a loss severity of 43.6 percent. This number is only modestly higher than the assumption used in forecasting the lifetime performance of the deal using the UBS methodology.

5. An overview of subprime MBS ratings

This section is intended to provide an overview of how the rating agencies assign credit ratings on tranches of a securitization. We start with a general discussion of credit ratings before moving into the details on the rating process. We continue with an overview of the process through which the credit rating agencies monitor performance of securitization deals over time, and review performance of credit ratings on securities secured by subprime mortgages. In this section there are a number of asides to complement the analysis: conceptual differences between corporate and structured credit ratings; a note on how through-the-cycle structured credit ratings can amplify the housing cycle; an explanation of the timing of recent downgrades.

5.1. What is a credit rating?

A credit rating by a CRA represents an overall assessment and opinion of a debt obligor's creditworthiness and is thus meant to reflect only credit or default risk. To be sure, it is not the obligor but the instrument issued by the obligor which receives a credit rating. The distinction is not that relevant for corporate bonds, where the obligor rating is commensurate with the rating on a senior unsecured instrument, but is quite relevant for structured credit products such as asset-backed securities (ABS). Nonetheless, in the words of a Moody's presentation (Moody's 2004), "[t]he comparability of these opinions holds regardless of the country of the issuer, is industry, asset class, or type of fixed-income debt." A recent S&P document states "[o]ur ratings represent a uniform measure of credit quality globally and across all types of debt instruments. In other words, an 'AAA' rated corporate bond should exhibit the same degree of credit quality as an 'AAA' rated securitized issue." (S&P 2007, p.4).

This stated intent implies that an investor can assume that, say, a double-A rated instrument is the same in the U.S. as in Belgium or Singapore, regardless whether that instrument is a standard corporate bond or a structured product such as a tranche on a collateralized debt obligation (CDO); see also Mason and Rosner (2007). The actual behavior of rated obligors or instruments may turn out to have more heterogeneity across countries, industries, and product types, and there is substantial supporting evidence. See Nickell, Perraudin, and Varvotto (2000) for evidence across countries of domicile and industries for corporate bond ratings, and CGFS (2005) for differences between corporate bonds and structured products.

The rating agencies differ about what exactly is assessed. Whereas Fitch and S&P evaluate an obligor's overall capacity to meet its financial obligation, and hence is best through of as an estimate of probability of default, Moody's assessment incorporates some judgment of recovery in the event of loss. In the argot of credit risk management, S&P measures PD (probability of default) while Moody's measure is somewhat closer to EL (expected loss) (BCBS, 2000).[15] Interestingly, these differences seem to remain for structured products. In describing their ratings criteria and methodology for structured products, S&P states: "[w]e base our ratings framework on the likelihood of default rather than expected loss or loss given default. In other words, our ratings at the rated instrument level don't incorporate any analysis or opinion on post-default recovery prospects." (S&P, 2007, p. 3) By contrast, Fitch incorporates some measure of expected recovery into their structured product ratings.[16]

Credit ratings issued by the agencies typically represent an unconditional view, sometimes called "cycle-neutral" or "through-the-cycle:" the rating agency's own description of their rating methodology broadly supports this view.

(Moody's 1999, p. 6-7) "...[O]ne of Moody's goals is to achieve stable *expected* [italics in original] default rates across rating categories and time ... Moody's believes that giving only modest weight to cyclical conditions serves the interests of the bulk of investors."

---

[15] Specifically, EL = PD×LGD, where LGD is loss given default. However, given the paucity of LGD data, little variation in EL exists at the obligor (as opposed to instrument) level can be attributed to variation in LGD making the distinction between the agencies modest at best.
[16] See http://www.fitchratings.com/corporate/fitchResources.cfm?detail=1&rd_file=intro#rtng_actn.

(S&P 2001, p. 41): "Standard & Poor's credit ratings are meant to be forward-looking; ... Accordingly, the anticipated ups and downs of business cycles – whether industry specific or related to the general economy – should be factored into the credit rating all along ... The ideal is to rate 'through the cycle'".

This unconditional or firm-specific view of credit risk stands in contrast to risk measures such as EDFs (expected default frequency) from Moody's KMV. An EDF has two principal inputs: firm leverage and asset volatility, where the latter is derived from equity (stock price) volatility. As a result EDFs can change frequently and significantly since they reflect the stock market's view of risk for that firm at a given point in time, a view which incorporates both systematic and idiosyncratic risk.

Unfortunately there is substantial evidence that credit rating changes, including changes to default, exhibit pro-cyclical or systematic variation (Nickell, Perraudin, and Varotto, 2000; Bangia et. al, 2002; Lando and Skodeberg, 2002), especially for speculative grades (Hanson and Schuermann, 2006).

5.2. How does one become a rating agency? [17]

Credit ratings have a long history of playing a role in the regulatory process going back to the 1930s in the U.S. (Sylla, 2002). Asset managers such as pension funds and insurers often have strict asset allocation guidelines which are ratings driven, such as, for instance, a ceiling on the amount that can be invested in speculative grade debt.[18] With the introduction of the Basel 2 standards, ratings have entered bank capital regulation. But whose ratings can be used is left up to the host country supervisor.[19] In the U.S. we use the SEC designation of a "Nationally Recognized Statistical Rating Organization," NRSRO, introduced in 1975. All three main rating agencies at the time – Moody's, S&P and Fitch – received this designation (White, 2002). It was not until 1997 that the SEC laid out formal criteria for becoming an NRSRO (Levich, Majnoni and Reinhart, 2002). Only with the Credit Rating Agency Reform Act of 2006 did the SEC officially obtain authority to regulate and supervise CRAs that have been designated NRSROs.[20]

Under the Reform Act, in order to qualify as an NRSRO, a credit agency must register with the SEC and it must have been in business as a credit rating agency for at least three consecutive years proceeding the date of its application.[21] The application must contain, among other things, information regarding the applicant's credit ratings performance measurement statistics over short-term, mid-term, and long-term periods; the procedures and methodologies that the applicant uses in determining credit ratings; policies or procedures adopted and implemented to prevent misuse of material, nonpublic information; and any conflict of interest relating to the issuance of credit ratings by the applicant.[22] All documentation submitted by the applicant

---

[17] We are indebted to Michelle Meertens for help with this section.
[18] ERISA, the Employee Retirement Income Security Act of 1974, is one such example.
[19] European guidelines can be found in "Committee of European Banking Supervisors, Guidelines on the Recognition of External Credit Assessment Institutions (Jan 20, 2006); available at http://www.bundesbank.de/download/bankenaufsicht/pdf/cebs/GL07.pdf.
[20] The final rule did not come out until June 2007 (http://www.sec.gov/rules/final/2007/34-55857fr.pdf).
[21] 15 U.S.C. 78c(a)(62).
[22] 15 U.S.C. 78o-7(a)(1)(B).

must be made publicly available on its website,[23] and the information must be kept up to date and current.[24]

Since the early 1970s (1970 for Moody's and Fitch, S&P a few years later), issuers rather than investors are charged for obtaining a rating. These ratings are costly: $25,000 for issues up to $500 million, ½ bp for issues greater than $500 million (Kliger and Sarig, 2000). Treacy and Carey (2000) report that the usual fee charged by S&P is 3.25 bp of the face amount, though it may be up to 4.25 bp (Tomlinson and Evans, 2007); Fitch charges 3-7 bp (Tomlinson and Evans, 2007). The fees charged for rating structured credit products are higher: up to 12 bp by S&P and 7-8 bp by Fitch (Tomlinson and Evans, 2007). Moody's does not publish its pricing schedule.

5.3. When is a credit rating wrong? How could we tell?

Highly rated firms default quite rarely. For example, Moody's reports that the one-year investment grade default rate over the period 1983-2006 was 0.073% or 7.3 bp. This is an average over four letter grade ratings: Aaa through Baa. Thus in a pool of 10,000 investment grade obligors or instruments we would expect seven to default over the course of one year. What if only three default? What about eleven? Higher than expect default could be the result of either a bad draw (bad luck) or an indicator that the rating is wrong, and it is very hard to distinguish between the two, especially for small probabilities (see also Lopez and Saidenberg, 2000). Indeed the use of the regulatory color scheme, which is behind the 1996 Market Risk Amendment to the Basel I, was motivated precisely by this recognition, and in that case the probability to be validated is comparatively large 1% (for 99% VaR) (BCBS, 1996) with daily data.

There are other approaches. Although rating agencies insist that their ratings scale reflects an ordinal ranking of credit risk, they also publish default rates for different horizons by rating. Thus we would expect default rates or probabilities to be monotonically increasing as one descends the credit spectrum. Using ratings histories from S&P, Hanson and Schuermann (2006) show formally that monotonicity is violated frequently for most notch-level investment grade one-year estimated default probabilities. The precision of the probability of default (PD) point estimates is quite low; see Appendix 3 for further discussion. Indeed there have been no defaults over one year for triple-A or AA+ (Aa1) rated firms, yet surely we do not believe that the one-year probability of default is identically equal to zero.

Although the one-year horizon is typical in credit analysis (and is also the horizon used in Basel 2), most traded credit instruments have longer maturity. For example, the typical CDS contract is five years, and over that horizon there are positive empirical default rates for Aaa and Aa1 which Moody's reports to be 7.8bp and 14.9bp respectively (Moody's, 2007c).

"We perform a very significant but extremely limited role in the credit markets. We issue reasoned, forward-looking opinions about credit risk," says Fran Laserson, vice president of corporate communications at Moody's. "Our opinions are objective and not tied to any recommendations to buy and sell."

---

[23] 15 U.S.C. 78o-7(a)(3).
[24] 15 U.S.C. 78o-7(b)(1).

5.4. The subprime credit rating process

The rating process can be split into two steps: (1) estimation of a loss distribution, and (2) simulation of the cash flows. With a loss distribution in hand, it is straightforward to measure the amount of credit enhancement necessary for a tranche to attain a given credit rating. Credit enhancement (CE) is simply the amount of loss on underlying collateral that can be absorbed before the tranche absorbs any loss. When a credit rating is associated with the probability of default, the amount of credit enhancement is simply the level of loss CE such that the probability that loss is higher than CE is equal to the probability of default.

Figure 9 below illustrates how one can use the portfolio loss distribution in order map the PD associated with a credit rating on a particular tranche to a level of credit enhancement required for that tranche. For example, given a PD associated with a AAA credit rating, the credit enhancement is quite high at CE(AAA). However, given a higher PD associated with a BBB credit rating, the required credit enhancement is much lower at CE(BBB). A better credit rating is achieved through greater credit enhancement.

In a typical subprime structure, credit enhancement comes from two sources: subordination and excess spread. Subordination refers to the par value of tranches with claims junior to the tranche in question relative to the par value of collateral. It represents the maximum level of loss that could occur immediately without investors in the tranche losing one dollar of interest or principal. Excess spread refers to the difference between the income and expenses of the structure. On the income side, the trust receives interest payments and prepayment penalties from borrowers. On the expense side, the trust pays interest on tranches to investors, pays a fee to the servicer, and might have other payments to make related to derivatives like interest rate swaps. In most structures, excess spread is captured for the first three to five years of the life of the deal, which increases the amount of subordination for each rated tranche over time. Determining how much credit excess spread can be given to meet the required credit enhancement is a dynamic problem that involves simulating cash flows over time, and is the second step of the rating process. We now discuss each of these two steps in greater detail.

Figure 9: Mapping the Loss Distribution to Required Credit Enhancement

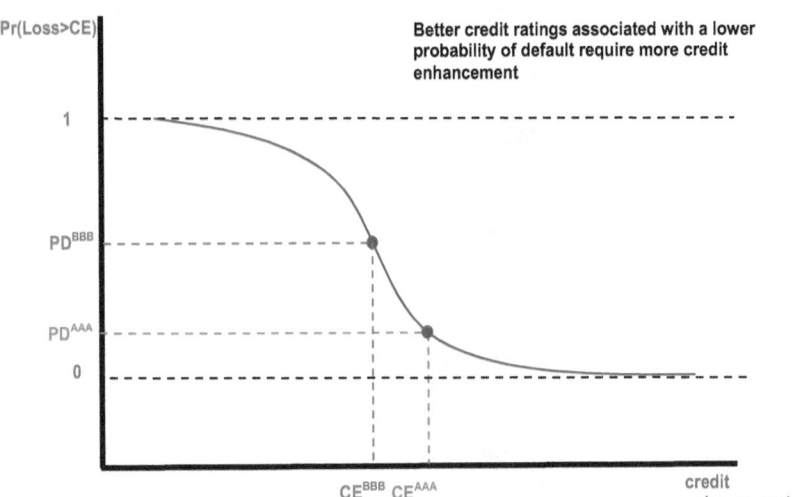

5.4.1. Credit enhancement

In the first step of the rating process, the rating agency estimates the loss distribution associated with a given pool of collateral. The mean of the loss distribution is measured through the construction of a baseline frequency of foreclosure and loss severity for each loan that depends on the characteristics of the loan and local area economic conditions. The distribution of losses is constructed by estimating the sensitivity of losses to local area economic conditions for each mortgage loan, and then simulating future paths of local area economic conditions.

In order to construct the baseline, the rating agency uses historical data in order to estimate the likely sensitivity of the frequency of foreclosure and severity of loss to underwriting characteristics of the loan, the experience of the originator and servicer, and local area and national economic conditions. Most of the agencies claim to rely in part on loan-level data from *LoanPerformance* over 1992-2000 in order to estimate these relationships.

The key loan underwriting characteristics include:

- cumulative loan-to-value ratio (CLTV)
- consumer credit score (FICO)
- loan maturity (15 years, 30 years, 40 years, etc)
- interest rate
- fixed-rate (FRM) vs. adjustable-rate (ARM)
- property type (single-family, townhouse, condo, multi-family)
- home value
- documentation of income and assets

- loan purpose (purchase, term refinance, cash-out refinance)
- owner occupancy (owner-occupied, investor)
- mortgage insurance
- asset class (Jumbo, Alt-A, Subprime)

The key originator and servicer adjustments include:

- past performance of the originator's loans
- underwriting guidelines of the mortgage loans and adherence to them
- loan marketing practices
- credit checks made on borrowers
- appraisal standards
- experience in origination of mortgages
- collection practices
- loan modification and liquidation practices

Table 21 documents how the credit support (the product of the frequency of foreclosure and loss severity) for a pool of mortgage loans is sensitive to changes in loan attributes.

Table 21: Sensitivity of Aaa Credit Enhancement Levels to Loan Attributes

	Sample Pool A		Sample Pool B	
	Aaa credit support	Change from Base	Aaa credit support	Change from Base
Base Pool	3.17		2.57	
LTV+5%	4.28	35%	3.52	37%
LTV-5%	2.32	-27%	1.85	-28%
FICO+20	3.02	-5%	2.49	-3%
FICO-20	3.42	8%	2.75	7%
All Cashout				
Appraisal Quality	4.68	48%	3.91	52%
All Purchase	2.62	-17%	2.15	-16%
All Investor	3.69	16%	2.99	16%
All 15-year term	2.42	-24%	1.93	-25%
All ARM	3.47	9%	2.81	9%
All Condo	3.31	4%	2.68	4%
All Alt Doc	3.35	6%	2.78	8%
Price > $300k, LTV constant	3.8	20%	3.10	21%

Source: *Moody's Mortgage Metrics*
Pool A: LTV 67, FICO 732, CashOut 19%, Purch 21%, Single Fam 89%, Owner 98%, Fulldoc 75%, 30-year 98%, Fixed Rate 100% Pool B: LTV 65, FICO 744, CashOut 17%, Purch 21%, Single Fam 89%, Owner 96%, Fulldoc 95%, 30-year 98%, Fixed Rate 100%

The Aaa credit enhancement for the base pools are illustrated in the first row. As Pool A has a higher LTV, lower FICO, and lower percentage of full documentation than Pool B, it has a higher level of credit support (3.17 percent versus 2.57 percent). Table 21 also illustrates the impact of changing one characteristic of the pool for all loans in the pool, holding all other characteristics constant. For example, if all loans in the pool were underwritten under an Alternative Documentation program, the credit support of Pool A would increase by 6 percent to 3.35 percent and Pool B would increase by 8 percent to 2.78 percent. Note that the change in support depends on both the sensitivity of support to the loan characteristic as well as the size of the change in the characteristic. Changes in leverage appear to have significant effects on credit support, as an increase of five percentage points is associated with an increase in credit support by more than one-third.[25]

The rating agency will typically adjust this baseline for current local area economic conditions like the unemployment rate, interest rates, and home price appreciation. The agencies are quite opaque about this relationship, and for some reason do not illustrate the impact of changes in local area economic conditions on credit enhancement in their public rating criteria. For example, Fitch employs scaling factors developed by University Financial Associates which control for four different components of regional factors: macro factors like employment rates and construction activity, demographic factors like population growth; political/legal factors; and even topographic factors that might constrain the growth of housing markets. The multipliers typically range from 0.5 to 1.7 and are updated quarterly.

In order to simulate the loss distribution, the rating agency needs to estimate the sensitivity of losses to local area economic conditions. Fitch tackles this problem by breaking out actual losses on mortgage loans into independent national and state components for each quarter. The sensitivity of losses to each factor is equal to one by construction. The final step is to fix a distribution for each of these components, and then simulate the loss distribution of the mortgage pool using random draws from the distribution of state and national components of unexpected loss.[26]

5.5. Conceptual differences between corporate and ABS credit ratings

Subprime ABS ratings differ from corporate debt ratings in a number of different dimensions:

- Corporate bond (obligor) ratings are largely based on firm-specific risk characteristics. Since ABS structures represent claims on cash flows from a *portfolio* of underlying assets, the rating of a structured credit product must take into account systematic risk. It is correlated losses which matter especially for the more senior (higher rated) tranches, and loss correlation arises through dependence on shared or common (or systematic) risk factors.[27] For ABS deals which have a large number of underlying assets, for instance MBS, the portfolio is large enough such that all idiosyncratic risk is diversified away leaving only systematic exposure to the risk factors particular to that product class (here, mortgages). By contrast, a substantial amount of idiosyncratic risk may remain in

---

[25] Note that Moody's have increased subordination levels in subprime RMBS by 30 percent over last three years, and this can be largely attributed to an increase in support required by a decline in underwriting standards.

[26] Note that Fitch actually simulates the frequency of foreclosure and loss severity separately, but the discussion here focuses on the product (expected loss) for simplicity. Each of the national and state components is likely transformed by subtracting the mean and dividing by the standard deviation, so that the distribution converges to a standard normal distribution. This permits the agency to use a two-factor copula model in order to simulate the loss distribution. Note that the sensitivity of losses to the normalized component would be equal to the inverse of the standard deviation of the actual component.

[27] Note that correlation includes more than just economic conditions, as it includes (a) model risk by the agencies (b) originator and arranger effects (c) servicer effects.

ABS transactions with smaller asset pools, for instance CDOs (CGFS, 2005; Amato and Remolona, 2005).

Because these deals are portfolios, the effect of correlation is not the same for all tranches: equity tranches prefer higher correlation, senior tranches prefer lower correlation (tail losses are driven by loss correlation). As correlation increases, so does portfolio loss volatility. The payoff function for the equity tranche is, true to its name, like a call option. Indeed equity itself is a call option on the assets of the underlying firm, and the value of a call option is increasing in volatility. If the equity tranche is long a call option, the senior tranche is short a call option, so that their payoffs behave in an opposite manner. The impact of increased correlation on the value of mezzanine tranches is ambiguous and depends on the structure of a particular deal (Duffie, 2007). By contrast, correlation with systematic risk factors should not matter for corporate ratings.

As a result of the portfolio nature of the rated products, the ratings migration behavior may also be different than for ordinary obligor ratings. Moody's (2007a) reports that rating changes are much more common for corporate bond than for structured product ratings, but the magnitude of changes (number of notches up- or downgraded) was nearly double for the structured products.

- Subprime ABS ratings refer to the performance of a static pool instead of a dynamic corporation. When a firm becomes distressed, it has the option to change its investment strategy and inject more capital. As long as a firm is deemed to be creditworthy during neutral economic conditions, it is reasonable to expect that the firm could take prompt corrective action in order to avoid defaulting on its debt during a transitory decline in aggregate or industry conditions. However, the pool of mortgages underlying subprime ABS is fixed, and investors do not expect an issuer to support a weakly-performing deal.

- Subprime ABS ratings rely heavily on quantitative models while corporate debt ratings rely heavily on analyst judgment. In particular, corporate credit ratings require the separation of a firm's long-run condition and competitiveness from the business cycle, the assessment of whether or not an industry downturn is cyclical or permanent, and determination about whether or not a firm could actually survive a pro-longed transitory downturn.

- Unlike corporate credit ratings, ABS ratings rely heavily on a forecast of economic conditions. Note that a corporate credit rating is based on the agency's assessment that a firm will default during neutral economic conditions (i.e. full employment at the national and industry level). However, the rating agency is unable to focus on neutral economic conditions when assigning subprime ABS ratings, because in the model, uncertainty about the level of loss in the mortgage pool is driven completely by changes in economic conditions. If one were to fix the level of economic activity – for example at full employment – the level of losses is determined, and according to the model, the probability of default is either zero or one. It follows that the credit rating on an ABS tranche is the agency's assessment that economic conditions will deteriorate to the point where losses on the underlying mortgage pool will exceed the tranche's credit enhancement. In other words, it is largely based on a forecast of economic conditions combined with the agency's estimated sensitivity of losses to that forecast.

- Finally, while an ABS credit rating for a particular rating grade should have similar expected loss to corporate credit rating of the same grade, the volatility of loss can be quite different across asset classes.

5.6. How through-the-cycle rating could amplify the housing cycle

Like corporate credit ratings, the agencies seek to make subprime ABS credit ratings through the housing cycle. Stability means that one should not see upgrades concentrated during a housing boom and downgrades concentrated during a housing bust.

It is not difficult to understand that changes in economic conditions affect the distribution of losses on a mortgage pool. The unemployment rate and home price appreciation have obvious effects on the ability of a borrower to avoid default and the severity of loss in the event of default.

Consider a AAA-rated tranche issued during an environment of high home price appreciation (HPA). Figure 10 illustrates that the level of credit enhancement is determined using the probability associated with a AAA credit rating and the rating agency's estimate of the loss distribution (blue) in this economic environment. However, as the housing market slows down, the loss distribution shifts to the right, as any level of probability is now associated with a higher level of loss. If the rating agency does not respond to this new loss distribution and uses the same level of credit enhancement to structure new deals in a tough economic environment, the probability of default associated with these AAA-rated tranche will actually be closer to a AA than a AAA. It follows that keeping enhancement constant through the cycle will result in ratings instability, with upgrades during a boom and downgrades during a bust.

Rating agency must respond to shifts in the loss distribution by increasing the amount of needed credit enhancement to keep ratings stable as economic conditions deteriorate, as illustrated in the Figure. It follows that the stabilizing of ratings through the cycle is associated with pro-cyclical credit enhancement: as the housing market improves, credit enhancement falls; as the housing market slows down, credit enhancement increases.

This phenomenon has two important implications:

- Pro-cyclical credit enhancement has the potential to amplify the housing cycle, creating credit and asset price bubbles on the upside and contributing to severe credit crunches and on the downside. In order to understand this point, consider the hypothetical example in Figure 11. On the left is an aggressive structure based on strong housing market conditions. The AAA tranche is 80 percent of the funding, and the weighted-average cost of funds is LIBOR+92 bp. However, as the housing market slows down, the rating agency removes leverage from the structure, and increases the subordination of the AAA-rated tranche from 20 to 25 percent. By requiring a larger fraction of the deal to be financed by BBB-rated debt, the weighted-average cost of funds increases to LIBOR+100 bp. This higher cost of funds will require higher interest rates on subprime

45

mortgage loans, or will require a significant tightening in underwriting standards on the underlying mortgage loans. Note that the de-leveraging the structure has a knock-on effect on economic activity by reducing the supply of credit. It is difficult at this point to assess the importance of this phenomenon to what appeared to be a bubble in housing credit and prices on the upside. One source of concern is that the ratio of upgrades to downgrades appeared to be fairly stable for home equity ABS over 2001-2006 (see the discussion on rating performance below). However, the impact on the downside is fairly certain. One week after a historical downgrade action by the agencies, leading subprime lenders discontinued offering the 2/28 and 3/27 hybrid ARM (see the discussion of ratings performance below).

- Investors in subprime ABS are vulnerable to the ability of the rating agency to predict turning points in the housing cycle and respond appropriately. One must be fair to note that the downturn in housing did not surprise the rating agencies, who had been warning investors about the possibility and the impact on performance for quite some time. However, it does not appear that the agencies appropriately measured the sensitivity of losses to economic activity or anticipated the severity of the downturn.

Figure 10: Credit enhancement and economic conditions

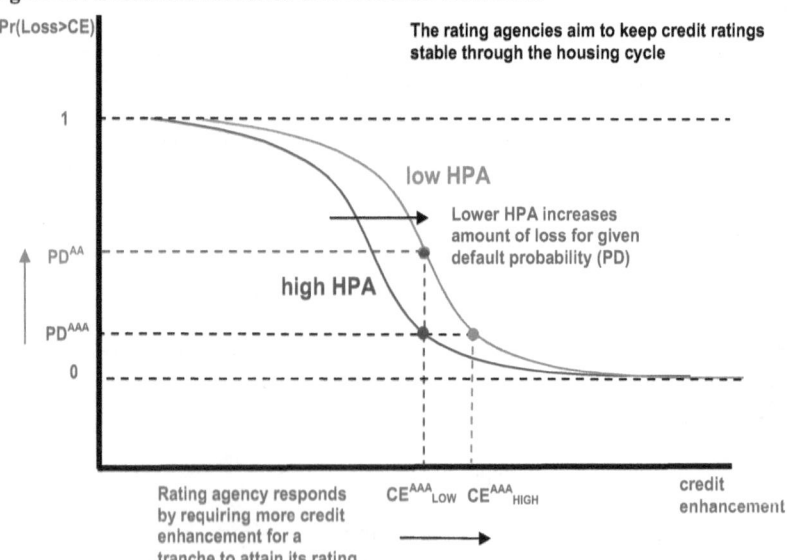

Figure 11: Procyclical credit enhancement

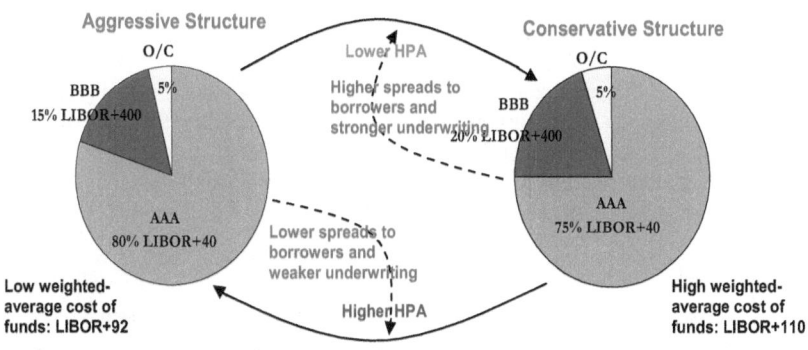

Contribute to a credit and house price bubble on the upside
Amplify the downturn and delay the recovery on the downside

5.7. Cash Flow Analytics for Excess Spread

The second part of the rating process involves simulating the cash flows of the structure in order to determine how much credit excess spread will receive towards meeting the required credit enhancement. As an example, in Table 22 we consider the credit enhancement corresponding to a hypothetical pool of subprime mortgage loans. In this example, the required credit enhancement for the Aaa tranche is 22.50%. A simulation of cash flows suggests that excess spread can contribute 9.25% to meet this requirement, suggesting that the amount of subordination for this tranche must be 13.25%. In this section, we briefly describe how the rating agencies measure this credit attributed to excess spread, focusing on subprime RMBS.

Table 22: Cash flow analytics

Tranche Rating	Required Credit Enhancement	Spread Credit	Subordination	Class Size
Aaa	22.50%	9.25%	13.25%	86.75%
Aa2	16.75%	9.25%	7.50%	5.75%
A2	12.25%	8.75%	3.50%	4.00%
Baa2	8.50%	8.50%	0.00%	3.50%
Total				100%
Source: Moody's				

The key inputs into the cash flow analysis involve:

- the credit enhancement for given credit rating
- the timing of these losses
- prepayment rates
- interest rates and index mismatches
- trigger events

- weighted average loan rate decrease
- prepayment penalties
- pre-funding accounts
- swaps, caps, and other derivatives.

The first input to the analysis is amount of losses on collateral that a tranche with a given rating would be able to withstand without sustaining a loss, which corresponds to the required credit enhancement implied from the loss distribution. Note that better credit ratings are associated with higher levels credit enhancement, and thus are associated with a higher level of expected loss on the underlying collateral.

The timing of losses

Table 23 illustrates Moody's assumption about the timing of losses, which is based on historical performance over 1993-1999. Note there are slight differences in the timing between fixed-rate and ARMs. Except for the first year, losses are assumed to be distributed evenly throughout the year. In the first year, losses are distributed evenly throughout the last six months. Adjustments to this assumption need to be made if the pool contains seasoned or delinquent loans.

Table 23: First-lien loss curve (as % of original pool balance)

Year	FRMs	ARMs
1	3%	3%
2	12%	17%
3	20%	25%
4	25%	25%
5	20%	20%
6	15%	10%
7	5%	0%
8	0%	0%
Total	100%	0%
Source: Moody's; based on historical performance over 1993-1999.		

Note that an acceleration in the timing of losses implies a lower level of excess spread in later periods, which reduces the contribution that excess spread can make to meet the required credit enhancement. It follows that a conservative approach to rating involves front-loading the timing of losses. Moreover, given the importance of the timing, it is possible to understand how the existence of elevated early payment defaults observed in the 2006 vintages of RMBS will correspond to significant adverse effects on the ratings performance.

Prepayment risk

Prepayments of principal include both the voluntary and involuntary (i.e. default) varieties. Note that the path of the dollar value of involuntary prepayments over time has been tied down by assumptions about the level and timing of losses. It follows that assumptions about the prepayment curve really just pin down the severity of loss on defaulted mortgages (in order to identify the number of involuntary prepayments) and the number of voluntary prepayments. Table 24 documents Moody's assumptions about prepayment rates for a Baa2-rated tranche secured by a portfolio of subprime loans. The standard measure of prepayment frequency is the Constant Prepayment Rate (CPR), defined as the annualized one-month prepayment rate of loans that remain in the pool.

Table 24: Pre-payment assumption for Baa2-rated tranches

Loan age (months)	FRMs	ARMs	2/28s	3/27s
1	6%	5.5%	5.5%	5.5%
2-18	↑ by 1.33%/mth	↑ by 1.639%/mth	↑ by 1.639%/mth	↑ by 1.639%/mth
19-24	30%	35%	33%	33%
25-30	30%	35%	55%	33%
31-36	30%	35%	33%	33%
37-42	30%	35%	33%	55%
43+	30%	35%	33%	33%

Source: Moody's

For both fixed-rate (FRMs) and adjustable-rate mortgages (ARMs), the CPR increases every month until the 19th month, where it stays constant through the remaining life of the deal. However, for hybrid ARMs, which have a fixed interest rate for either 2 or 3 years and then revert to an ARM, there is a spike in the CPR in the six months following payment reset. Note that since prepayments include defaults, it is necessary to adjust the prepayment curve for the credit rating of the tranche under analysis. Recall that a better credit rating is associated with a higher level of loss on collateral, which means a higher frequency of involuntary prepayments. Table 25 documents adjustments that Moody's makes to the CPR by rating category. For example, the prepayment rate is 15 percent higher for a Aaa-rated tranche than a Baa2-rated tranche in order to capture the higher frequency of involuntary prepayment (i.e. default) associated with the Aaa level of loss.

Table 25: Adjustments by tranche credit rating to Baa2 pre-payment curves

Rating	FRM	ARM
Aaa	133%	115%
Aa1	126%	112.5%
Aa2	120%	110%
Aa3	117%	108.5%
A1	113%	106.5%
A2	110%	105%
A3	107%	103.5%
Baa1	103%	101.5%
Baa2	100%	100%
Baa3	97%	98.5%
Ba1	93%	96.5%
Ba2	90%	95%
Ba3	87%	93.5%
B1	83%	91.5%
B2	80%	90%
B3	77%	88.5%

Source: Moody's

The assumptions made above identify the dollar value of involuntary prepayments and the total number of prepayments. In order to identify the number of involuntary prepayments (and consequently the number of voluntary prepayments), it is necessary to make an assumption about loss severity. Note that this assumption about severity is different from the one used in the determination of credit enhancement in the first step outlined above. Moody's makes the assumption that the fraction of involuntary prepayments in total prepayments increases with the severity of loss (i.e. as the credit rating improves). This phenomenon is described in Table 26.

Table 26: Loss Severity Assumptions for 1st lien subprime mortgages

Aaa	60%
Aa	55%
A	50%
Baa	45%
Ba	42.5%
B	40%

Source: Moody's

In the end, voluntary prepayments reduce principal and thus the benefit of excess spread. It follows that a conservative view toward rating will typically make high and front-loaded assumptions about the path of voluntary prepayments, as this reduces the contribution that excess spread makes towards credit enhancement.

Interest rate risk

The key remaining source of uncertainty in the analysis of cash flows is the behavior of interest rates. Note that the coupons on tranches typically have floating interest rates tied to the one-month LIBOR. Moreover, note that interest rates on some of the underlying loans are adjustable, which makes receipts from collateral vary with the level of interest rates. Interest rate risk is created by mis-matches between the sensitivity of collateral and tranches to interest rates. Some examples include:

- Fixed rate loans funded with floating rate certificates
- Prime rate index funded with LIBOR based certificates
- six-month LIBOR loans funded with one-month LIBOR certificates

Based on a number of factors, including the state of the economy, the forward-rate curve, and the current level of interest rates, interest rate stresses are determined.

Interest rate risk had an adverse impact on the performance of RMBS structures issued during the 2002 to 2004. In particular, throughout 2002 to mid-2004, the one-month LIBOR maintained a level to 1% - 1.8%. However, in June 2004, the one-month LIBOR began to increase quickly, reaching 5.3% in 2006. This increase in interest rates has an adverse impact through three channels. First, the coupons on ARM collateral adjust less quickly than the coupons on floating-rate certificates. Second, while rising rates will reduce the prepayment of fixed-rate loans, they also encourage a deterioration in the coupons on adjustable-rate loans as these obligors refinance out of high interest-rate loans, leaving a higher fraction of low- and fixed-interest rates in the pool. Finally, the increase in prepayment rates leads to quick return of principal to investors in senior tranches, where credit spreads are the smallest. Each of these factors leads to a compression of excess spread.

Many structures enter into an interest rate swap agreement which replaces the flexible-rate coupon paid to the tranches with a fixed-rate coupon in order to avoid this type of problem. However, note that this swap does not completely remove interest rate risk. For example, when pools contain ARM mortgages, the structure is vulnerable to a decline in interest rates which reduces the cash flows from collateral.

The approach of the rating agencies to interest rate risk is to construct a path of interest rate stresses in order to capture the worst likely movement in interest rates. Table 24 illustrates the interest rate stresses used by Fitch.

Table 27: Interest Rate Stresses

Month	Decreases from LIBOR				Increases from LIBOR			
	BBB	A	AA	AAA	BBB	A	AA	AAA
6	-1.06%	-1.24%	-1.42%	-1.68%	0.88%	1.40%	2.07%	3.10%
12	-1.81%	-2.09%	-2.37%	-2.76%	1.22%	2.02%	3.06%	4.66%
24	-2.28%	-2.68%	-3.08%	-3.64%	2.01%	3.15%	4.63%	6.90%
36	-2.52%	-2.95%	-3.39%	-4.00%	2.18%	3.43%	5.05%	7.53%
48	-2.52%	-2.97%	-3.43%	-4.09%	2.52%	3.85%	5.58%	8.24%
60	-2.52%	-2.98%	-3.45%	-4.12%	2.65%	4.02%	5.79%	8.52%

Source: Fitch (August 2007)

Note that these are changes (in percentage points) relative to the one-month LIBOR. The magnitude of the interest rate shocks is larger for better credit ratings and longer maturities.

Other details

Cash flow analysis is performed incorporating step-down triggers. For each rating level, the triggers are analyzed for the probability that they will be breached. As the triggers are set at levels which protect the rated tranches, they typically will be breached in stress scenarios. It follows that one typically assumes that the transaction does not step down (i.e. credit enhancement is not released) and that all tranches are paid sequentially for its life. Finally, mortgage loans with higher interest rates tend to prepay first, which reduces excess spread of the transaction over time. In order to capture this, Moody's assumes that the weighted average coupon (WAC) of the loans decreases by one basis point each month over the first three years of the deal.

Motivating example

In order to better understand the cash flow analysis, we will illustrate using a structure similar to GSAMP Trust 2006-NC2. In particular, we focus on a hypothetical pool of 2/28 ARM mortgage loans with an initial interest rate of 8 percent, a margin of 6 percent, and interest rate caps of 1.5%. The servicer receives a fee of 50 bp and master servicer receives a fee of 1 bp, each per annum and senior to any distributions to investors. The trust enters into an interest rate swap with a counterparty paying a fixed rate of 5.45% and receiving LIBOR – initially at 5.32% --according to a swap notional schedule described in Figure 8. Each month, the net payment to the swap counterparty is senior to any distributions to investors. Table 28 documents that the capital structure is similar to that of the New Century deal, but with fewer tranches in order to simplify the analysis.

Table 28: Capital Structure

Tranche	Width	Spread
AAA	79.35%	0.25%
AA	9.20%	0.31%
A	4.90%	0.37%
BBB	3.45%	1.00%
BB	1.70%	2.50%
O/C	1.40%	

Note: spread over 1-month LIBOR

We focus our analysis on the BBB-rated tranche. Our analysis starts with prepayment rates, which are illustrated in Figure 12. The total CPR is the fraction of remaining loans which prepay each month at an annualized rate, and is taken from Table 24 above for 2/28 ARMs. Notice the spike in prepayment rates shortly following payment rest at 24 months. The involuntary CPR is tied down by (a) the level of losses, assumed in this case to be 10% given the BBB rating; (b) the timing of losses documented in Table 23; (c) and the severity of losses from Table 26 in order to convert dollars of principal loss into an involuntary prepayment rate. Since the timing assumption precludes losses after 72 months, we only focus on the first six years of the deal life. As the capital structure of the deal is fixed, this exercise is essentially a test of whether or not the BBB-rated tranche as structured can receive a 6.9% credit (= 10% - 3.1%) from excess spread to meet the required credit enhancement.

Figure 12: Decomposing Constant Prepayment Rates (CPRs)

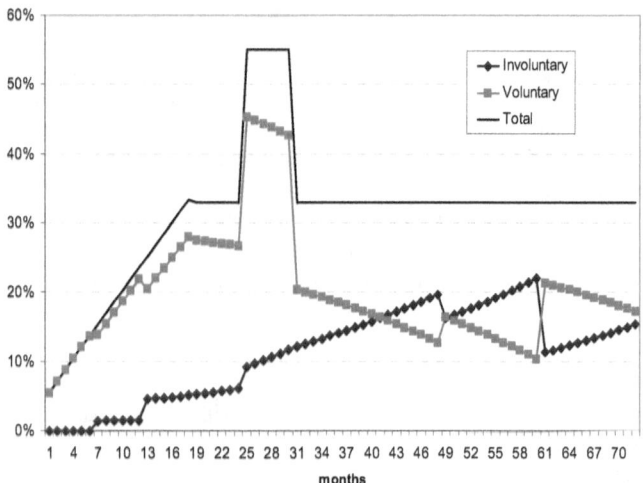

Figure 13: LIBOR stress, trust earnings, and the net swap payment

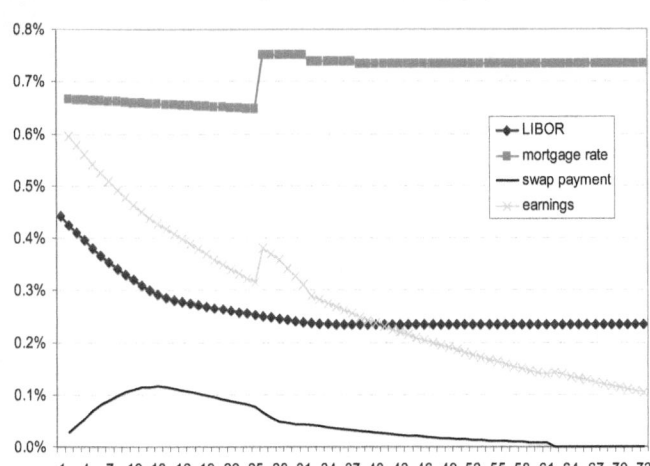

Note: the swap payment and earnings are each measured at a monthly rate and relative to original portfolio par. Earnings is defined as the difference between mortgage interest income, the net swap payment, and servicer fees of 51 basis points per annum.

Given the path of pre-payments, one needs to use the interest rate stresses in order to simulate future cash flows. Since the structure is hedged, the most severe interest rate shock is a decline in interest rates. When the interest rate on mortgages declines but the interest rate on tranches is fixed there is pressure on earnings. Figure 13 documents that assumed path of LIBOR, taken from Table 27 above, but converted into a monthly interest rate. The slow decrease over the first 24 months in the mortgage income reflects adverse selection in prepayment (high interest rates pre-paying first). There is an obvious spike in the mortgage interest rate at 24 months once payments reset. As LIBOR is falling, there is a net payment made to the swap counterparty, but this declines over time as the amount of swap notional goes to zero over the five-year life of the contract. The earnings of the trust before distributions and loss falls over time as mortgages prepay and the interest rate on remaining mortgages falls.

Figure 14: Earnings, Tranche Interest, and Credit Loss

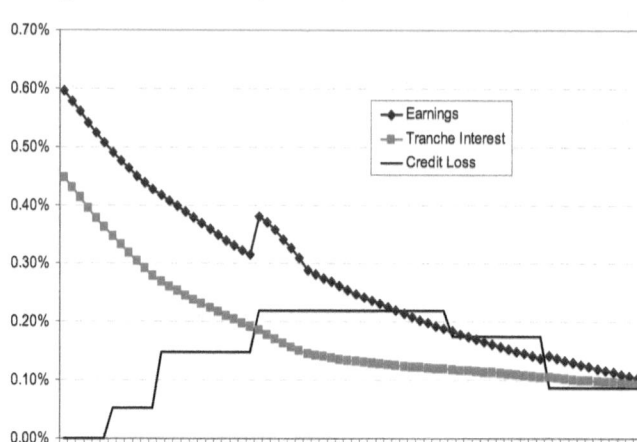

Note: Earnings, tranche interest, and credit loss are measured each at a monthly rate and relative to original portfolio par

Figure 14 documents the path of trust earnings, tranche interest, and credit losses over time, each measured at a monthly rate and relative to portfolio par. Tranche interest declines over time as interest rates fall and as pre-payments reduce the principal value of the senior tranche. While earnings are adequate to cover tranche interest initially, after the first year credit losses are eating into over-collateralization. After 42 months, earnings no longer cover losses, and the structure is struggling greatly.

Figure 15: Dynamic subordination of mezzanine tranches (10% required enhancement)

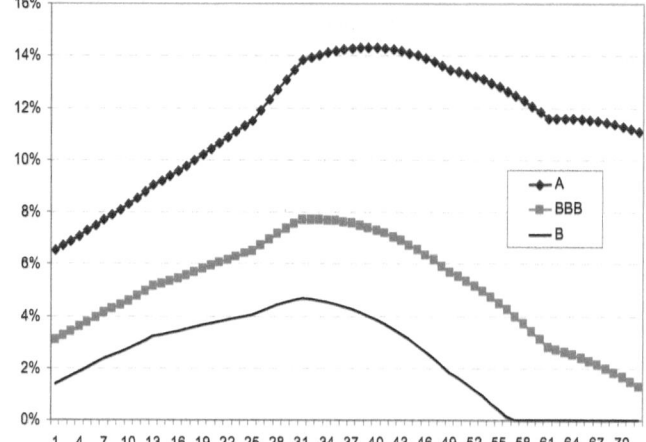

54

Figure 15 documents that these losses reduce the subordination available to each tranche over time. At 56 months, over-collateralization has been exhausted and the BB-rated tranche defaults. However, the BBB-rate tranche is able to survive until 72 months, suggesting that this tranche could withstand a loss rate of 10 percent. It follows that the deal is structured adequately.

Figure 16: Dynamic subordination of mezzanine tranches (10.5% required enhancement)

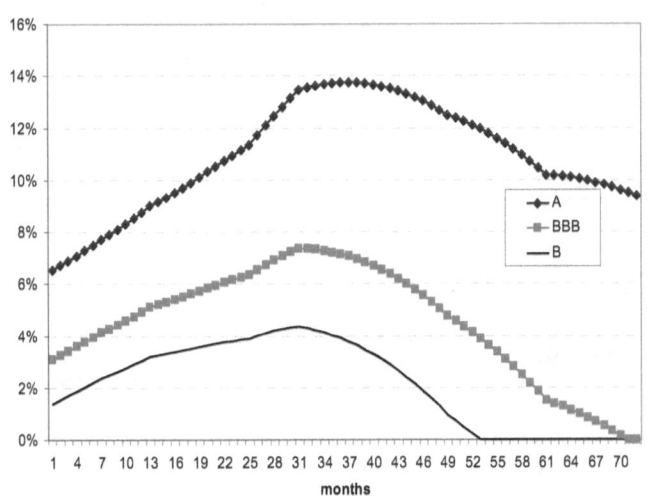

Figure 16 documents the dynamic subordination of the same capital structure in the event that losses are only 50 basis points higher. In this case, the BBB rated tranche defaults in month 70. The actual losses to investors in this tranche would be quite low because there are no losses after 72 months. However, when losses on the pool increase to 14%, the investors in the BBB-rated tranche are completely wiped out and the A-rated tranche defaults.

5.8. Performance Monitoring

The rating agencies currently monitor the performance of approximately 10,000 pools of mortgage loan collateral. Deal performance is tracked using monthly remittance from Intex Solutions, Inc. Since there is no uniform reporting methodology, the first step is to ensure the integrity of the data.

The agencies use this performance data in order to identify which deals merit a detailed review, but do complete such a review for every deal at least once a year. The key performance metric is the loss coverage ratio (LCR), which is defined as the ratio of the current credit enhancement for a tranche relative to estimated unrealized losses. Note that losses are estimated using underwriting characteristics for unseasoned loans (less than 12 months), and actual performance for seasoned loans. When the loss coverage ratio falls below an acceptable level given the rating of the tranche, the agency will perform a detailed review of the transaction, and consider ratings action.

In the example subprime deal described in Table 29, which is taken from a Fitch (2007) and does not correspond to the New Century deal, the pipeline measure of loss is constructed by applying historical default rates to the fraction of loans in each delinquency status bucket, and applying a projected loss severity. For example, the rating agency assumes that 68 percent of loans 90 days past due will default, while only 11 percent of current loans will default.

Table 29: Example of Projected Loss as a Percentage of Current Pool Balance

Status	Delinquency Status Distribution	Projected Default As % of Bucket	Projected Default As % of Pool	Projected Loss Severity	Expected Loss as % of Pool
Current	83	11	9.1	35	3.2
30 Days	4.0	37	1.5	35	0.5
60 Days	2.6	54	1.4	35	0.5
90 Days	2.5	68	1.7	35	0.6
Bankruptcies	1.7	54	0.9	35	0.3
Foreclosure	3.8	76	2.9	35	1.0
REO	2.6	100	2.6	35	0.9
Total	100.0		20.0	35	7.1

Notes: The example transaction is 18 months seasoned, has 63% of the original pool remaining (called the pool factor), incurred 0.77% loss to date, and reports a 60+ day of 13.15% (=2.6+2.5+1.7+3.8+2.6). The delinquency bucket figures (with the exception of REO) have a 98% home price appreciation adjustment applied. The example deal's current three-month loss severity is 25%, and the projected lifetime loss severity is approximately 35%. The expected loss figures are as a percentage of the remaining pool balance. The expected loss as a percentage of original pool balance is 5.25% = (7.1%*63%+0.77%)

The current subordination of a tranche reflects excess spread that has been retained as well as any losses to date. In this example in Table 30 the M-1 tranche rated AA currently has subordination of 20.61 percent. However, due to expected future accumulation of excess spread, this class can withstand losses of 26.90 percent, corresponding to a loss coverage ratio of 3.8 (= 26.9/7.1). Note that the target loss coverage ratio for the AA rating is 2.82, suggesting that the original rating is sound. However, the B-2 class rated BBB- currently has subordination of 3 percent and a break-loss rate of 10.41 percent. Note that the target break-loss for this rating is 11.04 percent, and the target break-loss of 9.95 for the BB+ rating (not reported). In this case, the rating agency is using tolerance to prevent this tranche from being downgraded at this time. A conversation with a ratings analyst suggested that a tranche would not be downgraded until it failed the target break-loss level for one full rating-grade below the current level.

Table 30: Example of Ratings Analysis Using Break-Loss Figures

Class	Current Rating	Current Subordination (%)	Current Break-Loss (%)	Current Loss Coverage Ratio (%)	Target Break-Loss (%)	Target Loss Coverage Ratio (%)	Model Proposed After Tolerances
A	AAA	31.59	39.71	5.61	27.18	3.84	AAA
M-1	AA	20.61	26.90	3.80	19.95	2.82	AA
M-2	A	12.08	18.25	2.58	15.79	2.23	A
M-3	BBB+	7.50	15.62	2.21	13.32	1.88	BBB+
B-1	BBB	5.92	13.14	1.86	12.09	1.71	BBB
B-2	BBB-	3.00	10.41	1.47	11.04	1.56	BBB-

Notes: The example transaction is 18 months seasoned and has a projected loss as a percent of current balance of 7.1%. Based on the projected delinquency, the triggers will pass at the step-down date and toggle thereafter. The current annualized excess spread available to cover losses is 3.10% (including interest rate derivatives). Current break-loss: the amount of collateral loss that would call the class to default. This figure includes excess spread and triggers. Current loss coverage ratio (LCR): determined by dividing the bond's current break-loss amount by the current base-case projected loss of 7.1%. Model proposed: Considers the difference between the current LCR and the target LCR

Figure 17: Anatomy of a downgrade

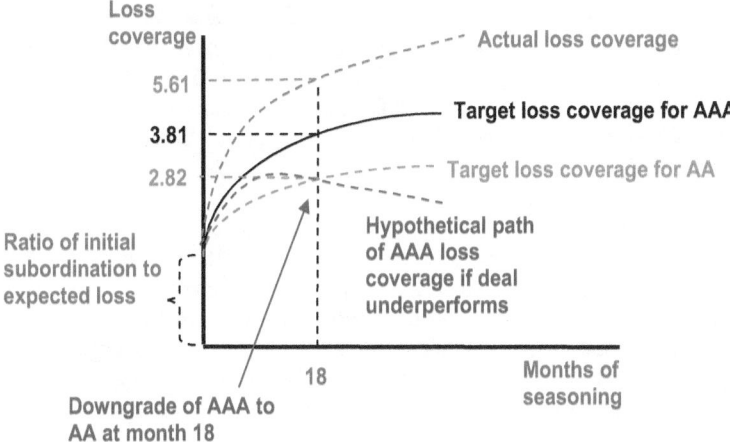

It is worth taking the time to highlight how changes in rating criteria affect the ratings monitoring process. In particular, if the rating agencies become more conservative in structuring new deals, it is not clear that anything should change when it comes to making a decision to downgrade securities secured by seasoned loans. The numerator of the loss coverage ratio is the current subordination of the tranche, which is unaffected by any change in criteria. The denominator is the estimated unrealized loss. Unless the rating agency also changes its mapping from current loan performance to the probability of default, or updates its view on loss severity, the key input into the ratings monitoring process is unchanged. In this sense, there is no need to change the way the agency monitors existing transactions. If an existing transaction was structured with inadequate initial subordination, the normal ratings monitoring process will pick this up and downgrade appropriately. In this sense, there is no need to update existing transactions.

5.9. Home Equity ABS rating performance

Table 31 documents the performance of Moody's Subprime RMBS over the last five years. The table documents downgrades in the top panel and upgrades in the bottom panel, broken out across first- and second-lien mortgage loans, as well as by origination year. Rating actions are measured by fraction of origination volume affected, the fraction of tranches affected, and the fraction of deals affected. The first observation to note is that by any measure, the rating agencies have appeared to struggle rating subprime deals throughout the period, as the ratio of downgrades to upgrades is larger than one. That being said, the recent performance of subprime RMBS ratings has been historically bad. The table documents that 92 percent of 1st-lien subprime deals originated in 2006 as well as 84.5 percent of 2nd-lien deals originated in 2005 and 91.8 percent of 2nd-lien deals originated in 2006 have been downgraded.

Note that half of all downgrades of tranches in the history of Home Equity ABS were made in the first seven months of 2007. About half of these were made during the week of 9 July, when Moody's downgraded 399 tranches. About two-thirds of these downgrades involved securitizations by four issuers who accounted for about one-third of 2006 issuance: New Century, WMC, Long Beach, and Fremont. Note that 86% of the downgraded tranches were originally rated Baa2 or worse, which meant that the notional amount downgraded was only about $9 billion. However, the ratings action affected just under 50 percent of 2006 1st-lien deals and almost two-thirds of 2005 2nd-lien deals, and the mean downgrade severity was 3.2 notches. Table 32 documents the ratings transition matrices for the 2005 and 2006 vintages across 1st and 2nd-lien status as of October 2007. It is clear from the table that ratings action has been concentrated in the mezzanine tranches, but there are some notable downgrades of Aaa-rated tranches in the 2006 vintage of 2nd-lien loans.

In addition to the ratings action, the rating agencies announced significant changes to rating criteria, and took a more pessimistic view on the housing market. At the time of the downgrade action, Moody's announced that it expected median existing family home prices to fall by 10 percent from the peak in 2005 to a trough at the end of 2008. The rating agency also significantly increased its loss expectations for certain flavors of sub-prime mortgages (hybrid ARMs, stated-income, high CLTV, first-time home-buyer), reduced the credit for excess spread, and adjusted its cash flow analysis to incorporate the likely impact of loan modifications.

In response to the historic rating action on subprime ABS during the week of 9 July 2007, the rating agencies were heavily criticized in the press about the timing. In particular, investors pointed to the fact that the ABX had been trading at very high implied spreads since February. Some examples of recent business press:

"A lot of these should be downgraded sooner rather than later," said Jeff Given at John Hancock Advisors LLC in Boston, who oversees $3.5 billion of mortgage bonds. The ratings companies may be embarrassed to downgrade the bonds, he said. "It's easier to say two years from now that you were wrong on a rating than it is to say you were wrong five months after you rated it." [*Bloomberg*, 29 June 2007]

"Standard & Poor's, Moody's Investors Service and Fitch Ratings are masking burgeoning losses in the market for subprime mortgage bonds by failing to cut the credit ratings on about $200 billion of securities backed by home loans...Almost 65 percent of the bonds in indexes that track subprime mortgage debt don't meet the ratings criteria in place when they were sold, according to data compiled by Bloomberg." [ibid]

In response, the rating agencies counter that their actions are justified.

"People are surprised there haven't been more downgrades," Claire Robinson, a managing director at Moody's, said during an investor conference sponsored by the firm in New York on June 5. "What they don't understand about the rating process is that we don't change our ratings on speculation about what's going to happen." Bloomberg, 10 July 2007]

From the description of the ratings monitoring process above, it is clear that for unseasoned loans, the rating agencies weight their initial expectations of loss heavily in computing lifetime expected loss on the vintage. While the 2006 vintage did show some early signs of trouble with early payment defaults (EPDs), it was not clear if this just reflected the impact of lower home price appreciation on investors using subprime loans to flip properties, or foreshadowed more serious problems.

Figure 17 documents that the increase in serious delinquencies on a month-over-month basis on the ABX 06-1 and 06-2 vintages was actually slowing down through the remittance report released at the end of April. Figure 18 documents that implied spreads on the ABX tranches retreated from their February highs through the end of May. However, the remittance report at the end of May suggested a reversal of this trend, as serious delinquency accelerated. This pattern was confirmed with the report at the end of June, and the ratings action came approximately two weeks after the June 25 report.

While the aggregated data helps the rating agencies tell a reasonable story, it is certainly possible that aggregation hides a number of deals that were long overdue for downgrade. Given the public rating downgrade criteria, this is a quantitative question that we intend to address with future empirical work.[28]

---

[28] Note that the rating agencies took another wave of rating actions on RMBS in October.

Figure 17: Change in Serious Delinquency on Mortgages Referenced by the ABX

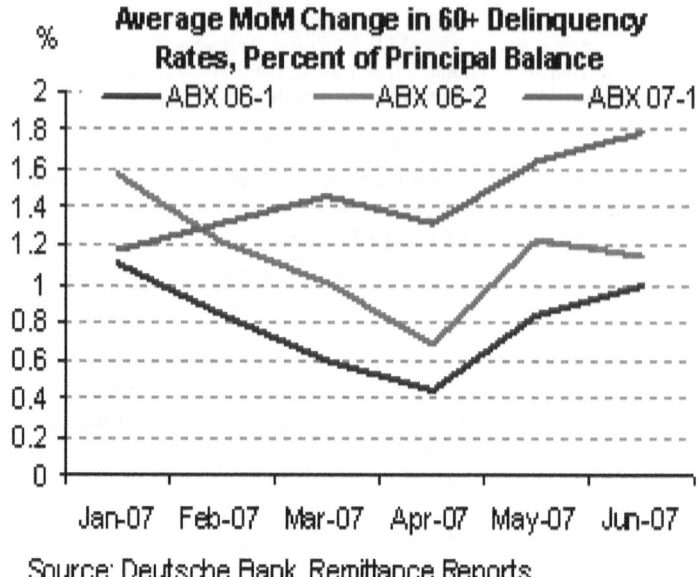

Figure 18: ABX Implied Spreads and Remittance Reporting Dates

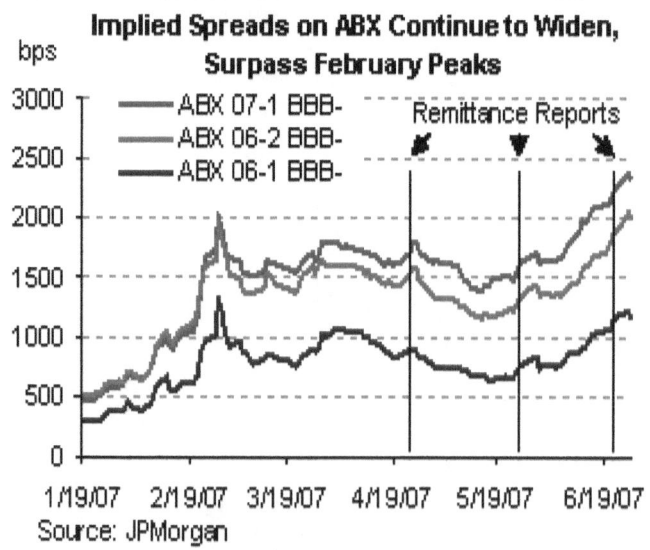

Table 31: Rating Changes in RMBS and Home Equity ABS, by Year

	Negative rating action								
	Subprime 1st lein			Subprime 2nd lein			Subprime all Lein		
Vintage	$	# tranche	# deals	$	# tranche	# deals	$	# tranche	# deals
2002	2.90%	13.80%	48.80%	1.50%	4.00%	9.10%	2.90%	13.20%	46.40%
2003	1.70%	10.10%	38.50%	0.70%	2.90%	11.10%	10.60%	9.60%	36.50%
2004	0.90%	6.20%	34.30%	1.70%	5.90%	44.00%	0.90%	6.20%	35.00%
2005	0.60%	3.60%	20.90%	3.30%	18.50%	85.40%	0.70%	4.90%	28.00%
2006	13.40%	48.00%	92.10%	60.00%	84.50%	91.80%	16.70%	52.30%	92.00%
	Positive rating action								
	Subprime 1st lein			Subprime 2nd lein			Subprime all Lein		
Vintage	$	# tranche	# deals	$	# tranche	# deals	$	# tranche	# deals
2002	2.10%	6.40%	20.80%	6.70%	17.30%	63.60%	2.30%	7.00%	23.50%
2003	2.80%	8.60%	26.40%	9.20%	30.10%	83.30%	2.90%	10.00%	30.50%
2004	1.20%	3.30%	15.00%	7.20%	22.30%	56.00%	1.40%	4.30%	17.90%
2005	0.00%	0.00%	0.00%	5.30%	9.60%	39.60%	0.20%	0.90%	4.40%
2006	0.00%	0.00%	0.00%	0.00%	0.00%	0.00%	0.00%	0.00%	0.00%

Source: Moodys (26 October 2007)

Table 32: Rating Transition Matrices

Current Rating/Last Rating (1st lein)											
2005	Aaa	Aa	A	Baa	Ba	B	Caa	Ca	C	Total	Down	Up
Aaa	100.00%									2,058	0	0
Aa		100.00%								983	0	0
A			99.40%	0.60%						1,003	6	0
Baa				94.90%	3.50%	1.40%	0.20%			1,066	54	0
Ba					81.10%	14.50%	4.40%			318	60	0

Current Rating/Last Rating (2nd lein)											
2005	Aaa	Aa	A	Baa	Ba	B	Caa	Ca	C	Total	Down	Up
Aaa	100.00%									113	0	0
Aa	22.00%	78.00%								100	0	22
A	0.90%	14.70%	81.90%	1.70%	0.90%					116	3	18
Baa				81.50%	9.60%	6.80%	1.40%	0.007		146	27	0
Ba				21.20%	34.80%	0.30%	0.273	0.136		66	52	0

Current Rating/Last Rating (1st lein)											
2006	Aaa	Aa	A	Baa	Ba	B	Caa	Ca	C	Total	Down	Up
Aaa	100.00%									2,121	0	0
Aa		100.00%								1,265	0	0
A			43.90%	27.90%	17.80%	10.10%	0.20%	0.001		1,295	726	0
Baa				17.30%	18.80%	32.40%	13.50%	0.111	0.07	1,301	1,076	0
Ba					6.20%	18.40%	8.20%	0.14	0.531	450	422	0

Current Rating/Last Rating (2nd lein)											
2006	Aaa	Aa	A	Baa	Ba	B	Caa	Ca	C	Total	Down	Up
Aaa	53.80%	34.90%	7.00%	4.30%						186	0	86
Aa		23.50%	38.80%	27.90%	6.60%	1.60%	0.50%	0.011		183	0	140
A			7.00%	32.60%	35.80%	11.80%	0.50%	0.064	0.059	187	0	174
Baa				5.60%	13.60%	17.80%	6.10%	0.145	0.425	214	0	202
Ba					1.00%	6.10%		0.051	0.879	99	0	98

Source: Moodys (26 October 2007)

6. The reliance of investors on credit ratings: A case study

A recent New York Times Editorial (08/07/2007) writes:

Protecting pensioners from bad investments will not be easy. A good place to start would be to make rating agencies more accountable, perhaps by asking regulators to monitor their quality. Many pension plans lack the analytical skills needed to evaluate these investments, relying on outside advisers and rating agencies. But the stellar triple-A rating assigned to many of these bonds proved to be misleading -- with the agencies now rushing to downgrade them.

In a recent Fortune article by Benner and Lachinsky (5 July 2007), Ohio Attorney General Marc Dann claims that the Ohio state pension funds have been defrauded by the rating agencies. "The ratings agencies cashed a check every time one of these subprime pools was created and an offering was made. [They] continued to rate these things AAA. [So they are] among the people who aided and abetted this continuing fraud." The authors note that Ohio has the third-largest group of public pensions in the United States, and that The Ohio Police & Fire Pension Fund has nearly 7 percent of its portfolio in mortgage- and asset-backed obligations:

Dann and a growing legion of critics contend that the agencies dropped the ball by issuing investment-grade ratings on securities backed by subprime mortgages they should have known were shaky. To his mind, the seemingly cozy relationship between ratings agencies and investment banks like Bear Stearns only heightens the appearance of impropriety.

In this section, we review the extent to which investors rely on rating agencies, focusing on the case of this Ohio pension fund, drawing upon on public disclosures of the fund.

- Overview of the fund
- Fixed-income investment guidelines
- Conclusions

6.1. Overview of the fund

The Ohio Police & Fire Pension Fund (http://www.op-f.org/) is a cost sharing multiple-employer public employee retirement system. The fund provides pension and disability benefits to qualified participants, survivor and death benefits as well as access to health care coverage for qualified spouses children, and dependent parents. In 2006, the fund had 912 participating employers from police and fire departments in Ohio municipalities, townships, and villages. Membership in the plan at the end of 2006 included 24,766 retired employees and 28,026 active employees. At the end of 2006, the fund had an investment portfolio of $11.2 billion. The fund's total rate of return was 16.15 percent in 2006 and 9.07 percent in 2005, each relative to an assumed actuarial rate of return of 8.25 percent.

Fund adequacy

The current actuarial analysis performed on the pension benefits reflects an "infinite" amortization period and a funding level of 78.3 percent. While the fund believes that the current funding status is strong, Ohio law requires that a 30-year amortization period is achieved.[29] A plan was approved by the Board and submitted to ORSC that included major changes to health care funding and benefits, and a recommendation that the legislature amend the law to provide for member contribution increases and employer contribution increases. However, the legislature has not taken action on the recommended contribution increases.

---

[29] Page ix in the 2006 Comprehensive Annual Financial Report, available at http://www.op-f.org/downloads/reports/CAFR2006.pdf.

Portfolio composition

Table 33 documents the exposure of the total fund to different asset classes. At the end of 2006, about 6.7% of total assets are invested in mortgages and mortgage-backed securities.

Table 33: Investment Portfolio

	2006		2005	
	($ m)	%	($ m)	%
Commercial Paper	594.6	5.03%	425.1	3.97
US Government Bonds	596.2	5.04	574.3	5.36
Corporate Bonds and Obligations	783.7	6.62	709.5	6.62
Mortgage & Asset Backed Obligations	799.4	6.76	734.6	6.85
Municipal Bonds		0.00	3.8	0.04
Domestic Stocks	2209.4	18.67	1967.7	18.36
Domestic Pooled Stocks	3181.9	26.89	2957.3	27.59
International Securities	2642.9	22.34	2328.2	21.72
Real Estate	658.	5.56	606.6	5.66
Commercial Mortgage Funds	73.3	0.62	80.4	0.75
Private Equity	291.9	2.47	230.2	2.15
Grand Total	11832.3	100.0	10717.9	100.0

Source: 2006 Comprehensive Annual Financial Report, Ohio Police & Fire Pension Fund

Table 34 documents the composition of the investment-grade fixed-income portfolio in 2006 and 2005. Non-agency MBS are likely included in the first four columns of the second row, which report the amount of mortgage and MBS broken out by credit rating. At the end of 2006, it appears that the fund held $740 million in non-agency MBS which had a credit rating of A- or better. Moreover, note that the share of non-agency MBS in the total fixed-income portfolio increased from 12% (245/2022) in 2005 to 34% (740/2179) in 2006. In other words, the pension fund almost tripled its exposure to non-agency MBS. Further, note that this increase in exposure to risky MBS was at the expense of exposure to MBS backed by full faith and credit of the United States government, or an agency or instrumentality thereof, which dropped from $489.6 million to $58.9 million.

Table 34: Fixed Income Investment Portfolio for 2006 [2005]

Rating of at least	A-	BBB-	B-	C-	Full Faith & Credit	Unrated	Total
Corporate Bond Obligations	$179.9 [$187.6]	$73.9 [$67.1]	$458.2 [$416.2]	$69.5 [$35.8]		$2.1 [$2.9]	$783.7 [$709.5]
Mortgage and ABS	$740.4 [$245.0]				$58.9 [$489.6]		$799.4 [$734.6]
Agency ABS	$37.7 [$3.8]						$37.7 [$3.8]
Munis	-- [$36.4]						-- [$36.4]
Treasury Strips					$62.3 [$29.4]		$62.3 [$29.4]
Treasury Notes					$496.1 [$508.5]		$496.1 [$508.5]
Total	$958.1 [$472.8]	$73.9 [$67.1]	$458.2 [$416.2]	$69.5 [$35.8]	$617.4 [$1027.5]	$2.1 [$2.9]	$2179.3 [$2022.3]

Source: 2006 Comprehensive Annual Financial Report, Ohio Police & Fire Pension Fund

In order to better understand the motivation for such a shift, consider Table 35, which illustrates spreads on the ABX and credit derivatives (CDS) by credit rating during 2006. While MBS backed by full faith and credit trade at close to zero credit spreads, securities secured by subprime loans pay significantly higher spreads.

Table 35: Subprime ABS vs. Corporate CDS Spreads

	June 2006		December 2006	
	ABX	CDS	ABX	CDS
AAA	18	11	11	9
AA	32	16	17	12
A	54	24	44	20
BBB	154	48	133	43

Source: ABX from Markit tranche coupon; CDS spread from Markit, average across US firms for 5-year contract with modified restructuring documentation clause.

6.2. Fixed-income asset management

From the investment guidelines in the 2006 annual report:

- The fixed-income portfolio has a target allocation of 18% of total fund assets, with a range of 13% to 23%. The portfolio includes investment grade securities (target of 12%), global inflation-protected securities (target of 6%), and commercial real estate (target of 0% and maximum of 2%).
- The investment grade fixed income allocation will be managed solely on an active basis in order to exploit the perceived inefficiencies in the investment grade fixed income markets.
- The return should exceed the return on the Lehman Aggregate Index over a three-year period on an annual basis.

- The total return of each manager's portfolio should rank above the median when compared to their peer group over a three-year period on an annualized basis and should exceed their benchmark return as specified in each manager's guidelines.

Mandates (from ORC Sec 742.11)

1. The main focus of investing will be on dollar denominated fixed income securities. Non-US dollar denominated securities are prohibited.
2. The composite portfolio as well as each manager's portfolio shall have similar portfolio characteristics as that of the Lehman Aggregate Index.
3. Issues must have a minimum credit rating of BBB- or equivalent at the time of purchase.
4. Each manager's portfolio has a specified effective duration band.
5. For diversification purposes, sector exposure limits exist for each manager's portfolio. In addition, each manager's portfolio will have a minimum number of issues.
6. Each manager's portfolio has a maximum threshold for the amount of cash that may be held at any one time.
7. Each manager's portfolio must have a dollar-weighted average quality of A or above.

Note that the Lehman Aggregate Index has a weight of less than one percent on non-agency MBS.

Asset management

In 2006, the fund's assets were 100% managed by external investment managers. The fixed-income group is comprised of eight asset managers who collectively have over $2.2 trillion in assets under management (AUM). They are (with AUM in parentheses):

- JPMorgan Investment Advisors, Inc. ($1.1 trillion, 2006)
- Lehman Brothers Asset Management ($225 billion, 2006)
- Bridgewater Associates ($165 billion, 2006)
- Loomis Sayles & Company, LP ($115 billion, 2006)
- MacKay Shields LLC ($40 billion, 2006)
- Prima Capital Advisors, LLC ($1.8 billion, 2006)
- Quadrant Real Estate Advisors LLC ($2.7 billion, 2006)
- Western Asset Management ($598 billion, 2007)

The 2005 performance audit of this fund suggested that investment managers in the core fixed income portfolio are compensated 16.3 basis points. The fund paid these investment managers approximately $1.304 million in 2006 in order to manage an $800 million portfolio of investment-grade fixed-income securities. While the 2006 financial statement reports that these managers out-performed the benchmark index by 26 basis points (= 459 - 433), this was accomplished in part through a significant reallocation of the portfolio from relatively safe to relatively risk non-agency mortgage-backed securities. One might note that after adjusting for the compensation of asset managers, this aggressive strategy netted the pension fund only 10 basis points of extra yield relative to the benchmark index, for about $2.1 million.

7. Conclusions

While this paper focuses on the securitization of subprime mortgages, many of the basic issues – intermediation and the frictions it introduces – are generic to the securitization process, regardless of the underlying pool of assets. The credit rating agencies play an important role in resolving or at least mitigating several of these frictions.

Our view is that the rating of securities secured by subprime mortgage loans by credit rating agencies has been flawed. There is no question that there will be some painful consequences, but we think that the rating process can be fixed along the lines suggested in the text above.

However, it is important to understand that repairing the securitization process does not end with the rating agencies. The incentives of investors and investment managers need to be aligned. The structured investments of investment managers should be evaluated relative to an index of structured products in order to give the manager appropriate incentives to conduct his own due diligence. Either the originator or the arranger needs to retain unhedged equity tranche exposure to every securitization deal. And finally, originators should have adequate capital so that warranties and representations can be taken seriously.

References

Aguesse, P. (2007). "Is Rating an Efficient Response to the Challenges of the Structured Finance Markets?" Risk and Trend Mapping No.2, Autorité des Marchés Financiers; available at http://www.amf-france.org/documents/general/7693_1.pdf.

Altman, E.I. and H.A. Rijken (2004). "How Rating Agencies Achieve Rating Stability." *Journal of Banking & Finance* 28, 2679-2714.

Amato, J.D. and E.M. Remolona (2005). "The Pricing of Unexpected Credit Losses." BIS Working Paper No. 190.

Bangia, A., F.X. Diebold, A. Kronimus, C. Schagen, and T. Schuermann (2002). "Ratings Migration and the Business Cycle, With Applications to Credit Portfolio Stress Testing." *Journal of Banking & Finance* 26: 2/3, 445-474.

Basel Committee on Banking Supervision (1996). "Amendment to the Capital Accord to Incorporate Market Risks." Basel Committee Publication No. 24. Available: www.bis.org/publ/bcbs24.pdf.

_____ (2000). "Credit Ratings and Complementary Sources of Credit Quality Information." BCBS Working Paper No. 3, available at http://www.bis.org/publ/bcbs_wp3.htm, August.

_____ (2005). "International Convergence of Capital Measurement and Capital Standards: A Revised Framework." Available at http://www.bis.org/publ/bcbs118.htm, November.

Cagan, Christopher (2007): "Mortgage Payment Reset," unpublished mimeo, May; available at http://www.facorelogic.com/landingpages/caganform.jsp?id=8037.

Cantor, R. and F. Packer (1995). "The Credit Rating Industry", *Journal of Fixed Income* 5:3 (December), 10-34.

Cantor, R. and C. Mann (2007). "Analyzing the Tradeoff between Ratings Accuracy and Stability." *Journal of Fixed Income* 16:4 (Spring), 60-68.

Committee on the Global Financial System (2005). "The Role of Ratings in Structured Finance: Issues and Implications." Available at http://www.bis.org/publ/cgfs23.htm, January.

Duffie, Darrell (2007), "Innovations in Credit Risk Transfer: Implications for Financial Stability," Stanford University GSB Working Paper, available at http://www.stanford.edu/~duffie/BIS.pdf.

The Economist (2007). "Measuring the Measurers." May 31.

_____ (2007). "Securitisation: When it goes wrong..." September 20.

Federal Reserve Board (2003). "Supervisory Guidance on Internal Ratings-Based Systems for Corporate Credit," Attachment 2 in http://www.federalreserve.gov/boarddocs/meetings/2003/20030711/attachment.pdf.

Fitch Ratings (2007): "U.S. Subprime RMBS/HEL Upgrade/Downgrade Criteria," Residential Mortgage Criteria Report, 12 July 2007.

Gourse, Alexander (2007): "The Subprime Bait and Switch," In These Times, July 16.

Hagerty, James and Hudson (2006): "Town's Residents Say They Were Targets of Big Mortgage Fraud," Wall Street Journal, September 27.

Hanson, S.G. and T. Schuermann (2006). "Confidence Intervals for Probabilities of Default." *Journal of Banking & Finance* 30:8, 2281-2301.

Inside Mortgage Finance (2007): "The 2007 Mortgage Market Statistical Annual."

Knox, Noelle (2006): "Ten mistakes that I made flipping a flop," USA Today, 22 October.

Kliger, D. and O. Sarig (2000). "The Information Value of Bond Ratings." *Journal of Finance*, 55:6, 2879-2902.

Lando, D. and T. Skødeberg (2002). "Analyzing Ratings Transitions and Rating Drift with Continuous Observations." *Journal of Banking & Finance* 26: 2/3, 423-444.

Levich, R.M., G. Majnoni, and C.M. Reinhart (2002). "Introduction: Ratings, Ratings Agencies and the Global Financial System: Summary and Policy Implications." In R.M. Levich, C. Reinhart, and G. Majnoni, eds. *Ratings, Rating Agencies and the Global Financial System*, Amsterdam, NL: Kluwer. 1-15.

Lopez, J.A. and M. Saidenberg (2000). "Evaluating Credit Risk Models." *Journal of Banking & Finance* 24, 151-165.

Mason, J.R. and J. Rosner (2007). "Where Did the Risk Go? How Misapplied Bond Ratings Cause Mortgage Backed Securities and Collateralized Debt Obligation Market Disruptions." Hudson Institute Working Paper.

Moody's Investors Services (1996). "Avoiding the 'F' Word: The Risk of Fraud in Securitized Transaction," Moody's Special Report, New York,

_____ (1999). "Rating Methodology: The Evolving Meanings of Moody's Bond Ratings." Moody's Global Credit Research, New York, August.

_____ (2003). "Impact of Predatory Lending an RMBS Securitizations," Moody's Special Report, New York, May.

_____ (2004). "Introduction to Moody's Structured Finance Analysis and Modelling." Presentation given by Frederic Drevon, May 13.

_____ (2005a). "The Importance of Representations and Warranties in RMBS Transactions," Moody's Special Report, New York, January.

_____ (2005b). "Spotlight on New Century Financial Corporation," Moody's Special Report, New York, July.

_____ (2007a). "Structured Finance Rating Transitions: 1983-2006." Special Comment, Moody's Global Credit Research, New York, January.

_____ (2007b) "Early Defaults Rise in Mortgage Securitization," Moody's Special Report, New York, January.

_____ (2007c). "Corporate Default and Recovery Rates: 1920-2006." Special Comment, Moody's Global Credit Research, New York, February.

_____(2007d). "Update on 2005 and 2006 Vintage U.S. Subprime RMBS Rating Actions: October 2007," Moodys Special Report, New York, October 26.

Morgan, Don (2007): "Defining and Detecting Predatory Lending," Staff Report #273, Federal Reserve Bank of New York.

New York Times (2007): "Pensions and the Mortgage Mess," Editorial, 7 August.

Nickell, P, W. Perraudin and S. Varotto, 2000, "Stability of Rating Transitions", *Journal of Banking & Finance*, 24, 203-227.

Scholtes, Saskia (2007). "Moody's alters its subprime rating model." *Financial Times*, September 25.

Sichelman, L. (2007). "Tighter Underwriting Stymies Refinancing of Subprime Loans." *Mortgage Servicing News*, May 1.

Smith, R.C. and I. Walter (2002). "Rating Agencies: Is there an Agency Issue?" in R.M. Levich, C. Reinhart, and G. Majnoni, eds. *Ratings, Rating Agencies and the Global Financial System*, Amsterdam, NL: Kluwer. 290-318.

Standard & Poor's (2001). "Rating Methodology: Evaluating the Issuer." Standard & Poor's Credit Ratings, New York, September.

_____ (2007). "Principles-Based Rating Methodology for Global Structured Finance Securities." Standard & Poor's RatingsDirect Research, New York, May.

Sylla, R. (2002). "An Historical Primer on the Business of Credit Rating." In R.M. Levich, C. Reinhart, and G. Majnoni, eds. *Ratings, Rating Agencies and the Global Financial System*, Amsterdam, NL: Kluwer. 19-40.

Thompson, Chris (2006): "Dirty Deeds," East Bay Express, July 23, 2007.

Tomlinson, R. and D. Evans (2007). "CDO Boom Masks Subprime Losses, Abetted by S&P, Moody's, Fitch." Bloomberg News, May 31.

Treacy, W.F. and M. Carey (2000). "Credit Risk Rating Systems at Large U.S. Banks." *Journal of Banking & Finance* 24, 167-201.

UBS Investment Research (26 June 2007): "Mortgage Strategist."

UBS Investment Research (23 October 2007): "Mortgage Strategist."

Wei, L (2007). "Subprime Lenders May Face Funding Crisis." *Wall Street Journal*, 10 January.

White, L. (2002). "The Credit Rating Industry: An Industrial Organization Analysis." in R.M. Levich, C. Reinhart, and G. Majnoni, eds. *Ratings, Rating Agencies and the Global Financial System*, Amsterdam, NL: Kluwer. 41-64.

Appendix 1: Predatory Lending

Predatory lending is defined by Morgan (2007) as the welfare-reducing provision of credit. In other words, the borrower would have been better off without the loan. While this practice includes the willful misrepresentation of material facts about a real estate transaction by an insider without the knowledge of a borrower, it has been defined much more broadly. For example, the New Jersey Division of Banking and Insurance (2007) defines predatory lending as an activity that involves at least one, and perhaps all three, of the following elements:

- Making unaffordable loans based on the assets of the borrower rather than on the borrower's ability to repay an obligation;
- Inducing a borrower to refinance a loan repeatedly in order to charge high points and fees each time the loan is refinanced ("loan flipping"); or
- Engaging in fraud or deception to conceal the true nature of the loan obligation, or ancillary products, from an unsuspecting or unsophisticated borrower.

Loans to borrowers who do not demonstrate the capacity to repay the loan, as structured, from sources other than the collateral pledged are generally considered unsafe and unsound. Some anecdotal examples of predatory lending:

Ira and Hazel purchased their home in 1983, shortly after getting married, financing their purchase with a loan from the Veterans' Administration. By 2002, they had nearly paid off their first mortgage. The elderly couple got a call from a lender, urging them to consolidate all of their debt into a single mortgage. The lender assured the husband who had excellent credit that the couple would receive an interest rate between 5-6% which would reduce their monthly mortgage payments. However, according to the couple, when the lender came to their house to have them sign the paperwork for their new mortgage, the lender failed to mention that the loan did not contain the low interest rate which they had been promised. Instead, it contained an interest rate of 9.9% and an annual percentage rate of 11.8%. Moreover, the loan contained 10 "discount points" ($15,289.00) which were financed into the loan, inflating the loan amount and stripping away the elderly couple's equity. Under the new loan, the monthly mortgage payments increased to $1,655.00, amounting to roughly 57% of the couple's monthly income. Moreover, the loan contained a substantial prepayment penalty, forcing them to pay approximately $7,500 to escape this predatory loan.
Source: Center for Responsible Lending (2007)

In 2005, Betty and Tyrone, a couple living on the south side of Chicago, took out a refinance loan with a lender in order to refurnish their basement. "We just kept asking them whether we were going to remain on a fixed rate, and they just kept lying to us, telling us we'd get a fixed rate," Betty alleges in a lawsuit against lender. As they later discovered, however, the terms of the loan were not as they expected. Not only did the loan have an adjustable rate that can go as high as 13.4 percent, but the couple allege that the lender falsely told them that their home had doubled in value since they had bought it a few years earlier, thus qualifying them for a larger loan amount. As the lender didn't give them copies of their loan documents at closing, and the couple did not realize that the terms had been changed until well after the three-day period during which they could legally cancel the loan. They have since tried to refinance, but have been unable to find another lender willing to lend them the amount currently owed, as the artificially-inflated appraisal value has in effect trapped them in a loan with a rising interest rate.
Source: Gourse (2007)

One scheme targets distressed borrowers at risk of foreclosure. The predator claims to the borrower that it is necessary to add someone else with good credit to the title, and their good credit will help secure a new loan on good terms. After the title holder uses the loan to make payments for a year, predator claims that the title would

be transferred back to the original borrower. However, predator cashes most of the remaining equity out of the house with a larger loan, and leaves the distressed borrower in a worse situation.
Source: Thompson (2006)

The Center for Responsible Lending has identified seven signs of a predatory loan:

- Excessive fees, defined as points and other fees of five percent or more of the loan
- Abusive prepayment penalties, defined as a penalty for more than three years or in an amount larger than six months interest
- Kickbacks to brokers, defined as compensation to a broker for selling a loan to a borrower at a higher interest rate than the minimum rate that the lender would be willing to charge
- Loan flipping, defined as the repeated refinancing of loans in order to generate fee income without any tangible benefit to the borrower
- Unnecessary products
- Mandatory arbitration requires a borrower to waive legal remedies in the event that loan terms are later determined to be abusive
- Steering and targeting borrowers into subprime products when they would qualify for prime products. Fannie Mae has estimated that up to half of borrowers with subprime mortgages could have qualified for loans with better terms

The role of the rating agencies

The rating agencies care about predatory lending to the extent that federal, state, and local laws might affect the amount of cash available to pay investors in residential mortgage-backed securitizations (RMBS) in the event of violations. Moody's analysis of RMBS transactions "includes an assessment of the likelihood that a lender might have violated predatory lending laws, and the extent to which violations by the lender would reduce the proceeds available to repay securitization investors" (Moody's, 2003).

In particular, Moody's requires that loans included in a securitization subject to predatory lending statutes satisfy certain conditions: (1) the statue must be sufficiently clear so that the lender can effectively comply; (2) the penalty to the trust for non-compliance is limited; (3) the lender demonstrates effective compliance procedures, which include a third-party review; (4) the lender represents that the loans comply with statutory requirements and agrees to repurchase loans that do not comply; (5) the lender indemnifies the trust for damages resulting from a particular statute; (6) the lender's financial resources and commitment to the business are sufficient to make these representations meaningful; and (7) concentration limits manage the risk to investors when penalties are high or statues are ambiguous.

Appendix 2: Predatory Borrowing:

While mortgage fraud has been around as long as the mortgage loan, it is important to understand that fraud becomes more prevalent in an environment of high and increasing home prices. In particular, when home prices are high relative to income, borrowers unwilling to accept a low standard of living can be tempted into lying on a mortgage loan application. When prices are high and rapidly increasing, there is an even greater incentive to commit fraud given that the cost of waiting is an even lower standard of living. Rapid home price appreciation also increases the return to speculative and criminal activity. Moreover, while benefits of fraud are increasing, the costs of fraud decline as expectations of higher future prices create equity that reduces the probability of default and severity of loss in the event of default.

In support of this claim, the IRS reports that the number of real-estate fraud investigations doubled between 2001 and 2003. Recent statistics from the FBI and Financial Crimes Network (FINCEN) document that suspicious activity reports (SARs) filed by federally-regulated institutions related to mortgage fraud have increased from 3,500 in 2000 to 28,000 in 2006. The Mortgage Asset Research Institute (2007) estimates that direct losses from mortgage fraud exceeded $1 billion in 2006, more than double the amount from 2005. The rapid slowdown in home price appreciation has made it more difficult to buy and sell houses quickly for profit, is quickly revealing the extent to which fraud permeated mortgage markets. For example, subprime and Alt-A loans originated in 2006 have experienced historical levels of serious early payment default (EPD), defined as being 90 days delinquent only three months after origination. Moody's (2007) notes that EPDs appear to be driven by borrowers using the loan to purchase for investment purposes, as opposed to borrowers refinancing an existing loan or purchasing a home for occupancy.

Predatory borrowing is defined as the willful misrepresentation of material facts about a real estate transaction by a borrower to the ultimate purchaser of the loan. This financial fraud might also involve cooperation of other insiders – realtors, mortgage brokers, appraisers, notaries, attorneys. The victims of this fraud include the ultimate purchaser of the loan (for example a public pension), but also include honest borrowers who have to pay higher interest rates for mortgage loans and prices for residential real estate. Below, I summarize the most common forms of predatory borrowing.

Fraud for housing

Fraud for housing constitutes illegal actions perpetrated solely by the borrower in order to acquire and maintain ownership of a home. This type of fraud is typified by a borrower who makes misrepresentations regarding income, employment, credit history, or the source of down payment. A recent example from Dollar (2006):

> A real estate agent would tell potential home buyers that they could receive substantial funds at closing under the guise of repair costs that they would be able to use for their personal benefit so long as they agreed to purchase certain "hard to sell" homes at an inflated price. Brokers would facilitate the submission of fraudulent loan applications for the potential homeowners that could not qualify for the loans. In some cases temporary loans were provided to buyers for down payments with the understanding they would be reimbursed at closing from the purported remodeling or repair costs, marketing services fees and other undisclosed disbursements. The buyers in those cases would falsely represent the sources of the down payments.

Fraud for profit

Fraud for profit refers to illegal actions taken jointly by a borrower and insiders to inflate the price of a property with no motivation to maintain ownership. The FBI generally focuses its effort on fraud perpetrated by industry insiders, as historically it involves an estimated 80 percent of all reported fraud losses. A recent example from Hagerty and Hudson (2006):

> The borrowers, who include truck drivers, factory workers, a pastor and a hair stylist, say they were duped by acquaintances into signing stacks of documents and didn't know they were applying for loans. Instead, they thought they were joining a risk-free "investment group." Now, many of the loans are in default, the borrowers' credit ratings are in ruins, and lenders are pursuing the organizers of the purported investment group in court. Companies stuck with the defaulting loans include Countrywide Financial Corp., the nation's largest home lender, and Argent Mortgage Co., another big lender. A lawsuit filed by Countrywide accuses the organizers of acquiring homes and then fraudulently selling them for a quick profit to the Virginia borrowers. Representatives of the borrowers put the total value of loans involved at about $80 million, which would make it one of the largest mortgage-fraud cases ever.

A summary by the Federal Bureau of Investigation of some popular fraud-for-profit schemes:

- Property flipping involves repeatedly selling a property to an associate at an artificially inflated price through false appraisals.
- A silent second the non-disclosure of a loaned down-payment to a first lien lender.
- Nominee loans involve concealing the true identify of the true borrower, who use the name and credit history of the of the nominee's name to qualify for a loan. The nominee could be a fictitious or stolen identity.
- Inflated appraisals involve an appraiser acts in collusion with a borrower and provides a misleading appraisal report to the lender.
- Foreclosure schemes involve convincing homeowners who are at risk of defaulting on loans or whose houses are already in foreclosure to transfer their deed and pay up-front fees. The perpetrator profits from these schemes by re-mortgaging the property or pocketing fees paid by the homeowner.
- Equity skimming involves the purchase of a property by an investor through a nominee, who does not make any mortgage payments and rents the property until foreclosure takes place several months later.
- Air Loans involve a non-existent property loan where a broker invents borrowers and properties, establishes accounts for payments, and maintains custodial accounts for escrows.

Source: Federal Bureau of Investigation

The role of the rating agencies

(Moody's, 1996) claim that the vast majority of all securitizations are tightly structured to eliminate virtually all fraud risk. The risk of fraud is greatest when
structures and technology developed for large, established issuers are mis-applied to smaller, less experienced issuers. Moreover, the lack of third-party monitors or involvement of entities with little or no track record increases the risk of fraud. The authors identify three potential types of fraud in a securitization:

- borrower fraud: the misrepresentation of key information during the application process by the borrower
- fraud in origination: misrepresentation of assets by the originator before securitization occurs, resulting in assets which do not conform with transaction's underwriting standards

- servicer fraud: the deliberate diversion, commingling, or retention of funds that are otherwise due to investors; the risk most significant among unrated, closely-held servicers that operate without third-party monitoring.

ComFed is a historical example of fraud in a mortgage securitization:

The parties involved at ComFed exaggerated property values to increase the volume-oriented commissions that they received for originating loans. To increase underwriting volumes still more, ComFed employees granted loans to unqualified borrowers by concealing the fact that these obligors had financed down payments with second-lien mortgages.

To prevent such instances of lower-level fraud, the originator's entire underwriting process should be reviewed to ensure that marketing and underwriting capacities remain entirely separate. Personnel involved in credit decisions should report to executives who are not responsible for marketing or sales. Underwriters' compensation should not be tied to volume; rather, if an incentive program is in place, the performance of the originated loans should be factored into the level of compensation.

(Moody's, 1996) claim that exposure to fraud can be minimized by the following:
- determine the integrity and competence of the management of the seller/servicer of a transaction through due diligence and background checks
- complete a thorough review of the underwriting process, including lines of reporting and employee compensation, to eliminate interests conflicting with those of investors
- establish independent third part monitoring of closely held entities with little external accountability that originate or service assets
- consider internal and external factors that could influence a servicer's conduct during the life of a securitization

This statement makes it clear that it is largely the responsibility of investors to conduct their own due diligence in order to avoid becoming victims of fraud.

Investors do receive a small but important amount of protection against fraud from representations and warranties made by the originator. Standard provisions protect investors from misinformation regarding loan characteristics, as well as guard against risks such as fraud, previous liens, and/or regulatory noncompliance.

(Moody's, 2005a) documents that an originator's ability to honor it obligation is the crucial component in evaluating the importance of these warranties. An investment grade credit rating often suffices to meet this standard. Otherwise, the rating agency claims that it will review established practices and procedures in order to ensure compliance and adequate tangible net worth relative to the liability created by the representations and warranties.

Appendix 3: Some Estimates of PD by Rating

A credit rating at a minimum provides an ordinal risk ranking: an AAA rating is better (in the sense of lower likelihood of default and loss) than an AA rating which is better than a BBB rating, and so on. More useful, however, is a cardinal ranking which would assign a numerical value such as a PD to each rating. Roughly speaking obligor PDs increase exponentially as one descends the credit spectrum.

The three major rating agencies have seven broad rating categories as well as rating modifiers, bringing the total to 19 rating classes, plus 'D' (default, an absorbing state[30]) and 'NR' (not rated – S&P, Fitch) or 'WR' (withdrawn rating – Moody's).[31] Typically ratings below 'CCC', e.g. 'CC' and 'C', are collapsed into 'CCC', reducing the total ratings to 17.[32] Although the rating modifiers provide a finer differentiation between issuers within one letter rating category, an investor may suffer a false sense of accuracy. Empirical estimates of *PD*s using credit rating histories can be quite noisy, even with over twenty-five year years of data. Under the new Basel Capital Accord (Basel 2), U.S. regulators would require banks to have a minimum of seven non-default rating categories (FRB, 2003).

A detailed discussion of PD accuracy is given in Hanson and Schuermann (2006), but in Table 36 we provide smoothed one-year PD estimates using S&P ratings histories from 1981-2006 for their global corporate obligor base. We present estimates at both the grade and notch level. Guided by the results Hanson and Schuermann (2006), we assign color codes to the PD estimates reflecting their estimation accuracy, with green being accurate, yellow moderately and red not accurate.[33] Hanson and Schuermann, using a shorter sample period (1981-2002), show that 95% confidence intervals of notch-level PD estimates are highly overlapping for investment grades (AAA through BBB-) but not so for speculative grades (BB through CCC). Since the point estimates for investment grade ratings are very small, a few basis points or less, it is effectively impossible to statistically distinguish the PD for an AA-rated obligor from an A-rated one. Indeed the new Basel Capital Accord, perhaps with this in mind, has set a lower bound of 3bp for any PD estimate (BCBS 2005, §285), commensurate with about a single-A rating.

---

[30] One consequence of default being an absorbing state arises when a firm re-emerges from bankruptcy. They are classified as a new firm.
[31] The CCC (S&P) and Caa (Moody's) ratings contain all ratings below as well – except default, of course. Fitch uses the same labeling or ratings nomenclature as S&P.
[32] Sometimes a C rating constitutes a default in which case it is included in the 'D' category. For no reason other than convenience and expediency, we will make use of the S&P nomenclature for the remainder of the paper.
[33] Accurate (green) means that adjacent notch-level PDs are statistically distinguishable, moderately accurate (yellow) means that PDs two notches apart are distinguishable, and not accurate (red) means that PDs two notches apart are not distinguishable (but may be so three or more notches apart).

Rating Categories	Smoothed PD estimates (notch level)	Smoothed PD estimates (grade level)[34]
AAA	0.02	0.02
AA+	0.06	
AA	0.6	0.8
AA-	1.3	
A+	1.8	
A	1.9	2.1
A-	2.1	
BBB+	4.4	
BBB	8.0	8.5
BBB-	12.6	
BB+	22.5	
BB	40.1	51.9
BB-	71.3	
B+	145	
B	540	368
B-	964	
CCC[35]	3,633	3,633

Table 36: S&P one-year PDs in basis points (1981 – 2006), global obligor base. Each entry is the average of two approaches: cohort based on monthly migration matrices and duration or intensity based.

---

[34] Note that grade level PD estimates for a given grade, say AA, need not be the same as the mid-point of the notch level PD estimate because a) PDs increase non-linearly (in fact approximately exponentially) as one descends the ratings spectrum, and b) the obligor distribution is uneven across (notch-level) ratings.
[35] Includes all grades below CCC.

www.ingramcontent.com/pod-product-compliance
Lightning Source LLC
Chambersburg PA
CBHW022129170526
45157CB00004B/1808